Frederick Philip Grove

OVER

Introduction: Malcolm Ross

PRAIRIE

General Editor: Malcolm Ross

TRAILS

New Canadian Library No. 1

McCLELLAND AND STEWART LIMITED

The following dedication appeared in the original edition:

THESE PAGES WERE WRITTEN FOR

MY WIFE

AND MY LITTLE DAUGHTER

TO READ BY THE EVENING FIRESIDE

The Canadian Publishers

McClelland and Stewart Limited

25 Hollinger Road, Toronto 374

PRINTED AND BOUND BY
T. H. BEST PRINTING COMPANY LIMITED

INTRODUCTION

I

*O*ver *Prairie Trails* was written by a man born in Russia of mixed Swedish, Scottish and English blood. Educated in Paris, Munich and Rome, twenty-one years of age before he came to this country after tours (large if not grand) from the Sahara to Madagascar to the Antipodes to America, Frederick Philip Grove is yet the typical, perhaps even the archetypal, Canadian. Certainly the fact of his thirty years with us before his first book (*this* book) was published in 1922 by McClelland and Stewart will overbear any narrowly technical scruples some might have about the man's nationality. However, Grove's was no mere passport Canadianism. He was not just a writer who happened to be writing in Canada. He was a *Canadian writer,* wholly absorbed by the Canadian scene and by the pioneer drama of a diverse yet single people; wholly convinced that this scene, this people, could yield to the artist's vision themes and values at once unique and universal.

The first thing that strikes one on re-reading *Over Prairie Trails* is Grove's almost incredible love for the harsh, punishing, desolate Manitoba land. Grove would have agreed, I think, that this land was harsh (but not therefore the less to be loved). And he was to bear its cruel marks to the grave. He would never, though, have conceded that word "desolate," despite these many lonely ventures over the winter waste of the prairie. For Grove—in season and out—the prairie is wonderfully alive. He exults in "the silver grey, leathery foliage which is so characteristic of our native woods." In his "beautiful wilderness" he watches for the "wavy flight" of the goldfinch and hears the whir of a whip-poor-will "shooting slantways upwards in its low flight."—"When I come to the home of frog and toad, or gartersnake and owl and whip-poor-will, a great tenderness takes possession of me, and I should like to shield and help them all and tell them not to be afraid of me." He regularly saves snippets of bacon for a gaunt prairie-wolf who meets him as by appointment on each of his return trips. Every twist and scar of the land is known and wondered at and claimed. Every freak of fog and drift and frost is a mighty event, to be known as the scientist tries to know but also to be felt, to be re-created and re-set in the "interior landscape" of the self. Grove is able to possess this northern world because he is first willing to be possessed by it. Note his rebuke to that misplaced person, the school janitor, "a highly efficient but exceedingly bad-humoured Cockney who was dissatisfied with all things Canadian because 'in the old country we do things differently.'"

Perhaps the fact that he knew so many lands and cultures saved Grove from being tied by homesick illusions to any one of them. Certainly he gave himself utterly to the pioneer challenge of "the fresh start," to a people as various as the people of his travels, and to the need (and the joy) of doing things differently.

Over Prairie Trails is the book of a man who is at home, not just "over here."

I have lived in southern countries, and I have travelled rather far for a single lifetime. . . . But then I was young. When the years began to pile up, I longed to stake off my horizons, to flatten out my views. . . . The parrot that flashed through "nutmeg groves" did not hold out so much allurement as the simple grey-and-slaty junco. The things that are unobtrusive and differentiated by shadings only—grey in grey above all —like our northern woods, like our sparrows, our wolves—they held a more compelling attraction than orgies of colour and screams of sound. So I came home to the north.

That recurrent but unobtrusive word "our" is no affectation.

II

Over Prairie Trails is a set of sketches describing seven trips between Gladstone and Falmouth near the western shore of Lake Manitoba. Desmond Pacey, in his critical study *Frederick Philip Grove*, gives us the circumstances. After a severe attack of pneumonia complicated by pleurisy, Grove had regained health sufficiently to accept the principalship of the Gladstone school (this was in 1916), "but his health henceforth was always uncertain."

Another source of anxiety was his developing awareness of the conflict between his aspirations as a writer and the necessity of remaining in the more secure profession of teaching in order properly to support his wife and daughter. During these four years as a teacher he had produced a negligible amount of writing; and his hopes of saving money on which to retire were further than ever from realization. As a step towards the solution of this economic problem, Mrs. Grove suggested that she should return to teaching, abandoned since the birth of their daughter. Accordingly for the school year 1917–18 she applied for and was granted a small school in a pioneer district thirty-four miles north of Gladstone.

During that year of separation, Grove visited his wife and daughter thirty-six times. He says of the seven drives here recorded that they "seem, as it were, lifted above the mass of others as worthy to be described in some detail." But do not let him cheat you into thinking of

these sketches as mere factual reports of drives that just
happened to be more memorable than the others. A fine
poetic craft has gone into the selection and deployment
of the facts (although facts they unquestionably are).
How easily these seven drives over the selfsame terrain
might have blurred into each other. Grove has the art of
being able to repeat without seeming to. He makes use
of the musical strategy of "theme and variations," giving
to each variation its own appropriate key and mood and
contriving within each a skilful set of modulations.

The first drive, in late September, is made in daylight,
twilight and moonlight. We *see* the trails, the wild life,
the scattered houses of the settlers. The little world between Gladstone and Falmouth is mapped out, the landmarks fixed. On later drives we are to feel Grove's sense
of relief when these landmarks suddenly loom up out of
fog or blizzard. On this first drive we meet the prairie
wolf, we bird-watch, we examine trees and bushes, and
the vagaries of the trail itself. And in the houses we pass,
Grove gives up a glimpse of frontier life.—"A house has
a physiognomy as well as a man, for him who can read
it; and this one, notwithstanding its new and shining
paint, was sullen, morose, and nearly vicious and spiteful. . . . I should not have cared to work for its owner."
Soon, this one.—"But this was prosperous, open-
handed, well-to-do middle class; not that conspicuous
'moneyedness' that we so often find in our new west
when people have made their success; but that solid,
friendly everyday liberality that for generations has not
had to pinch itself. . . ." And then this.—"Something
loomed up in front. Dark and sinister it looked. . . .
Between the silent grove to the south and the large,
whispering, wailing bluff to the north there stood in a
little clearing a snow-white log house, uncannily white in
the paling moonlight. I could still distinctly see that its
upper windows were nailed shut with boards—and, yes,

its lower ones, too. And yet, the moment I passed it, I saw, through one unclosed window on the north side, light. Unreasonably I shuddered." There is dread as well as magic on the trail.

And now the variations—the change of key. We follow the trail next in blind marsh-fog. The ear and the nose search out signs and landmarks. And fantasy is king. "No wonder, I thought, that the Northerners in their land of heath and bog were the poets of elves and goblins and of the fear of ghosts. Shrouds were these fogs, hanging and waving and floating shrouds! Mocking spirits were plucking at them and setting them into their gentle motions."

The third drive is keyed to silence and the stuff of dreams. Snow mutes the runners of the cutter. "We glided along over the virgin snow which had come soft-footedly over night, in a motion so smooth and silent as to suggest wingless flight." This is the poetry of silences. "Do you know which is the stillest hour of the night?" Through that still hour he travels until dawn comes as the breaking open of a dream: "And last I saw." The landscape, too, dreams under the snow, nature's "greatest equalizer." Now "there was no longer the raw, offending scar on Nature's body; just a smooth expanse of snow-white ribbon that led afar."

The fourth and fifth drives are charged with storm, bitter cold, terror. Here is the "pre-Adamic" world of violence. "I still remember . . . the foreboding that I had challenged a force in Nature which might defy all tireless effort and the most fearless heart." Here are weird "bomb-proof" sculptures of snow and ice in battle formation, drifts that lift horses and cutter over the tops of trees, winds that burrow and burn through the furs and under the skin.

"Speed" is the key for the sixth drive. His child is sick. He has no eye or ear for the scene now. The trail is sensed only in images of motion. "The distance seems to stand still, while the foreground rushes past you. The whole countryside seems to become a revolving, horizontal wheel with its hub at the horizon."

And the last drive is under the sky—the Manitoba sky of huge stars, chameleon clouds and the vaulting, moody northern lights. We *see* again. But we look up.

This tour de force of theme and variations (I have, of course, given only the broad pattern) is a carefully structured work. And never were Grove's senses keener, his powers of observation more evident. He has left us a memorable portrait of the "vanishing prairie." Here is lore for the naturalist and the historian—but shaped and held in the hand of the artist. Here, too, is the portrait of a man; over these lonely trails Grove, always in search of himself, for once found himself. No one, surely, will deny to this first book its permanent place in our literature.

MALCOLM ROSS

Queen's University,
    January, 1957

OVER PRAIRIE TRAILS

AUTHOR'S PREFACE

A FEW years ago it so happened that my work—teaching school—kept me during the week in a small country town in the centre of one of the prairie provinces while my family—wife and little daughter—lived in the southern fringe of the great northern timber expanse, not very far from the western shore of a great lake. My wife—like the plucky little woman she is—in order to round off my far-from-imperial income had made up her mind to look after a rural school that boasted of something like a residence. I procured a buggy and horse and went "home" on Fridays, after school was over, to return to my town on Sunday evening—covering thus, while the season was clement and allowed straight cross-country driving, coming and going, a distance of sixty-eight miles. Beginning with the second week of January this distance was raised to ninety miles because, as my more patient readers will see, the straight cross-country roads became impassable through snow.

These drives, the fastest of which was made in somewhat over four hours and the longest of which took me nearly eleven—the rest of them averaging pretty well up between the two extremes—soon became what made my life worth living. I am naturally an outdoor creature— I have lived for several years "on the tramp"—I love Nature more than Man—I take to horses—horses take to me—so how could it have been otherwise? Add to this that for various reasons my work just then was not of the most pleasant kind—I disliked the town, the town disliked me, the school board was sluggish and unprogressive, there was friction in the staff—and who can wonder that on Fridays, at four o'clock, a real holiday started for me: two days ahead with wife and child, and going and coming—the drive.

I made thirty-six of these trips: seventy-two drives in all. I think I could still rehearse every smallest incident of every single one of them. With all their weirdness, with all their sometimes dangerous adventure—most of them were made at night, and with hardly ever any regard being paid to the weather or to the state of the roads—they stand out in the vast array of memorable trifles that constitute the story of my life as among the most memorable ones. Seven drives seem, as it were, lifted above the mass of others as worthy to be described in some detail—as not too trivial to detain for an hour or so a patient reader's kind attention. Not that the others lack in interest for myself; but there is little in them of that mildly dramatic, stirring quality which might perhaps make their recital deserving of being heard beyond my own frugal fireside. Strange to say, only one of the seven is a return trip. I am afraid that the prospect of going back to rather uncongenial work must have dulled my senses. Or maybe, since I was returning over the same road after an interval of only two days, I had exhausted on the way north whatever there was of noticeable impressions to be garnered. Or again, since I was coming from "home," from the company of those for whom I lived and breathed, it might just be that all my thoughts flew back with such an intensity that there was no vitality left for the perception of the things immediately around me.

Chapter 1

FARMS AND ROADS

At ten minutes past four, of an evening late in September, I sat in the buggy and swung out of the livery stable that boarded my horse. Peter, the horse, was a chunky bay, not too large, nor too small; and I had stumbled on to him through none of my sagacity. To tell the plain truth, I wanted to get home, I had to have a horse that could stand the trip, no other likely-looking horse was offered, this one was; on a trial drive he looked as if he might do, and so I bought him—no, not quite—I arranged with the owner that I should make one complete trip with him and pay a fee of five dollars in case I did not keep him. As the sequence showed, I could not have found a better horse for the work in hand.

I turned on to the road leading north, crossed the bridge, and was between the fields. I looked at my watch and began to time myself. The moon was new and stood high in the western sky; the sun was sinking on the downward stretch. It was a pleasant, warm fall day, and it promised an evening such as I had wished for on my first drive out. Not a cloud showed anywhere. I did not urge the horse; he made the first mile in seven and a half minutes, and I counted that good enough.

Then came the turn to the west; this new road was a correction line, and I had to follow it for half a mile. There was no farmhouse on this short bend. Then north for five miles. The road was as level as a table top—a good, smooth, hard-beaten, age-mellowed prairie-grade. The land to east and west was also level; binders were going and whirring their harvest song. Nobody could have felt more contented than I did. There were two clusters of buildings—substantial buildings—set far back from the road, one east, the other one west, both clusters huddled homelike and sheltered in bluffs of planted cottonwoods, straight rows of them, three, four trees deep. My horse kept trotting leisurely along, the wheels kept turning, a meadow lark called in a desultory way from a nearby fence post. I was "on the go." I had torn up my roots, as it were, I felt detached and free; and if both these prosperous-looking farms had been my property—I believe, that moment a "Thank-you" would have bought them from me if parting from them had been the price of the liberty to proceed. But, of course, neither one of them ever could have been my property, for neither by temperament nor by profession had I ever been given to the accumulation of the wealth of this world.

A mile or so farther on there stood another group of farm buildings—this one close to the road. An unpainted barn, a long and low, rather ramshackle structure with sagging slide-doors that could no longer be closed, stood in the rear of the farmyard. The dwelling in front of it was a tall, boxlike two-story house, well painted in a rather loud green with white door and window frames. The door in front, one window beside it, two windows above, geometrically correct, and stiff and cold. The house was the only green thing around, however. Not a tree, not a shrub, not even a kitchen garden that I could see. I looked the place over critically, while I drove by. Somehow I was convinced that a bachelor owned it—a man who made this house—which was much too large for him—his "bunk." There it stood, slick and cold, inhospitable as ever a house was. A house has its physiognomy as well as a man, for him who can read it; and this one, notwithstanding its new and shining paint, was sullen, morose, and nearly vicious and spiteful. I turned away. I should not have cared to work for its owner.

Peter was trotting along. I do not know why on this first trip he never showed the one of his two most prominent traits—his laziness. As I found out later on, so long as I drove him single (he changed entirely in this respect when he had a mate), he would have preferred to be hitched behind, with me between the shafts pulling buggy and him. That was his weakness, but in it there also lay his strength. As soon as I started to dream or to be absorbed in the things around, he was sure to fall into the slowest of walks. When then he heard the swish of the whip, he would start with the worst of consciences, gallop away at breakneck speed, and slow down only when he was sure the whip was safe in its socket. When we met a team and pulled out on the side of the road, he would take it for granted that I desired to make conversation. He stopped instantly, drew one hindleg up, stood on three legs, and drooped his head as if he had come from the ends of the world. Oh yes, he knew how to spare himself. But on the other hand, when it came to a tight place, where only an extraordinary effort would do, I had never driven a horse on which I could more confidently rely. What any horse could do, he did.

About two miles beyond I came again to a cluster of buildings, close to the corner of the crossroads, sheltered, homelike, inviting, in a large natural bluff of tall, dark-green poplars. Those first two houses had had an aristocratic aloofness—I should not have liked to turn in there for shelter or for help. But this was prosperous, open-handed, well-to-do middle class; not that conspicuous "moneyedness" that we so often find in our new west when people have made their success; but the solid, friendly, everyday liberality that for generations has not had to pinch itself and therefore has mellowed down to taking the necessities and a certain amount of

give and take for granted. I was glad when on closer
approach I noticed a school embedded in the shady
green of the corner. I thought with pleasure of children
being so close to people with whom I should freely have
exchanged a friendly greeting and considered it a privi-
lege. In my mental vision I saw beeches and elms and
walnut trees around a squire's place in the old country.

The road began to be lined with thickets of shrubs
here: chokecherry bushes, with some ripe, dried-up
black berries left on the branches, with iron-black bark,
and with wiry stems, in the background; in front of them,
closer to the driveway, hawthorn, rich with red fruit;
rosebushes with scarlet leaves reaching down to nearly
underfoot. It is one of the most pleasing characteristics
of our native thickets that they never rise abruptly.
Always they shade off through cushionlike copses of
smaller growth into the level ground around.

The sun was sinking. I knew a mile or less farther
north I should have to turn west in order to avoid rough
roads straight ahead. That meant doubling up, because
some fifteen miles or so north I should have to turn east
again, my goal being east of my starting place. These
fifteen or sixteen miles of the northward road I did not
know; so I was anxious to make them while I could see.
I looked at the moon—I could count on some light from
her for an hour or so after sundown. But although I
knew the last ten or twelve miles of my drive fairly well,
I was also aware of the fact that there were in it tricky
spots—forkings of mere trails in muskeg bush—where
leaving the beaten log-track might mean as much as
being lost. So I looked at my watch again and shook the
lines over Peter's back. The first six miles had taken me
nearly fifty minutes. I looked at the sun again, rather
anxiously. I could count on him for another hour and a
quarter—well and good then!

There was the turn. Just north of it, far back from

both roads, another farmyard. Behind it, to the north, stretched out a long windbreak of poplars, with a gap or a vista in its centre. Barn and outbuildings were un-painted, the house white; a not unpleasing group, but something slovenly about it. I saw with my mind's eye numerous children, rather neglected, uncared-for, an overworked, sickly woman, a man who was bossy and harsh.

The road angles here. Bell's farm consists of three quartersections; the southwest quarter lends its diagonal for the trail: I had hardly made the turn, however, when a car came to meet me. It stopped. The school-inspector of the district looked out. I drew in and returned his greeting, half annoyed at being thus delayed. But his very next word made me sit up. He had that morning inspected my wife's school and seen her and my little girl; they were both as well as they could be. I felt so glad that I got out of my buggy to hand him my pouch of tobacco, the which he took readily enough. He praised my wife's work, as no doubt he had reason to do, and I should have given him a friendly slap on the shoulder, had not just then my horse taken it into his head to walk away without me.

I believe I was whistling when I got back to the buggy seat. I know I slapped the horse's rump with my lines and sang out, "Get up, Peter, we still have a matter of nearly thirty miles to make."

The road becomes pretty much a mere trail here, a rut track, smooth enough in the rut, where the wheels ran, but rough for the horse's feet in between.

To the left I found the first untilled land. It stretched far away to the west, overgrown with shrub-willow, wolf-willow and symphoricarpus—a combination that is hard to break with the plough. I am fond of the silver grey, leathery foliage of the wolf-willow which is so characteristic of our native woods Cinquefoil, too, the

shrubby variety, I saw in great numbers—another one
of our native dwarf shrubs which, though decried as a
weed, should figure as a border plant in my millionaire's
park.

And as if to make my enjoyment of the evening's
drive supreme, I saw the first flocks of my favourite bird,
the goldfinch. All over this vast expanse, which many
would have called a waste, there were strings of them,
chasing each other in their wavy flight, twittering on the
downward stretch, darting in among the bushes, turning
with incredible swiftness and sureness of wing the
shortest of curves about a branch, and undulating away
again to where they came from.

To the east I had, while pondering over the beautiful
wilderness, passed a fine bluff of stately poplars that
stood like green gold in the evening sun. They sheltered
apparently, though at a considerable distance, another
farmhouse; for a road led along their southern edge,
lined with telephone posts. A large flock of sheep was
grazing between the bluff and the trail, the most appropriate kind of stock for this particular landscape.

While looking back at them, I noticed a curious trifle.
The fence along my road had good cedar posts, placed
about fifteen feet apart. But at one point there were two
posts where one would have done. The wire, in fact, was
not fastened at all to the supernumerary one, and yet
this useless post was strongly braced by two stout, slanting poles. A mere nothing, which I mention only because
it was destined to be an important landmark for me on
future drives.

We drove on. At the next mile-corner all signs of
human habitation ceased. I had now on both sides that
same virgin ground which I have described above. Only
here it was interspersed with occasional thickets of
young aspen-boles. It was somewhere in this wilderness
that I saw a wolf, a common prairie-wolf with whom I

became quite familiar later on. I made it my custom during the following weeks, on my return trips, to start at a given point a few miles north of here eating the lunch which my wife used to put up for me: sandwiches with crisply fried bacon for a filling. And when I saw that wolf for the second time, I threw a little piece of bacon overboard. He seemed interested in the performance and stood and watched me in an averted kind of way from a distance. I have often noticed that you can never see a wolf from the front, unless it so happens that he does not see you. If he is aware of your presence, he will instantly swing around, even though he may stop and watch you. If he watches, he does so with his head turned back. That is one of the many precautions the wily fellow has learned, very likely through generations of bitter experience. After a while I threw out a second piece, and he started to trot alongside, still half turned away; he kept at a distance of about two hundred yards to the west, running in a furtive, half guilty-looking wày, with his tail down and his eye on me. After that he became my regular companion, an expected feature of my return trips, running with me every time for a while and coming a little bit closer till about the middle of November he disappeared, never to be seen again. This time I saw him in the underbrush, about a hundred yards ahead and as many more to the west. I took him by surprise, as he took me. I was sorry I had not seen him a few seconds sooner. For, when I focused my eyes on him, he stood in a curious attitude: as if he was righting himself after having slipped on his hindfeet in running a sharp curve. At the same moment a rabbit shot across that part of my field of vision to the east which I saw in a blurred way only, from the very utmost corner of my right eye. I did not turn but kept my eyes glued to the wolf. Nor can I tell whether I had stirred the rabbit up, or whether the wolf had been chasing or stalking it. I should have liked to know, for I have never seen a wolf stalking a rabbit, though I have often seen him stalk fowl. Had he pulled up when he saw me? As I said, I cannot tell, for now he was standing in the characteristic wolf-way, half turned, head bent back, tail stretched out nearly horizontally. The tail sank, the whole beast seemed to shrink, and suddenly he slunk away with amazing agility. Poor fellow—he did not know that many a time I had fed some of his brothers in cruel winters. But he came to know me, as I knew him; for whenever he left me on later drives, very close to Bell's corner, after I had finished my lunch, he would start right back on my trail, nose low, and I have no doubt that he picked up the bits of bacon which I had dropped as tidbits for him.

I drove and drove. The sun neared the horizon now. It was about six o'clock. The poplar thickets on both sides of the road began to be larger. In front the trail led towards a gate in a long, long line of towering cottonwoods. What was beyond?

It proved to be a gate indeed. Beyond the cottonwoods there ran an eastward grade lined on the north side by a ditch which I had to cross on a culvert. It will henceforth be known as the "twelve-mile bridge." Beyond the culvert the road which I followed had likewise been worked up into a grade. I did not like it, for it was new and rough. But less did I like the habitation at the end of its short, one-mile career. It stood to the right, close to the road, and was a veritable hovel.* It was built

---

* It might be well to state expressly here that, whatever has been said in these pages concerning farms and their inhabitants, has intentionally been so arranged as not to apply to the exact localities at which they are described. Anybody at all familiar with the district through which these drives were made will readily identify every natural landmark. But although I have not consciously introduced any changes in the landscape as God made it, I have in fairness to the settlers entirely redrawn the superimposed man-made landscape.

of logs, but it looked more like a dugout, for stable as well as dwelling were covered by way of a roof with blower-thrown straw. In the door of the hovel there stood two brats—poor things!

The road was a trail again for a mile or two. It led once more through the underbrush-wilderness interspersed with poplar bluffs. Then it became by degrees a real "high-class" Southern Prairie grade. I wondered, but not for long. Tall cottonwood bluffs, unmistakably planted trees, betrayed more farms. There were three of them, and, strange to say, here on the very fringe of civilization I found that "moneyed" type—a house, so new and up-to-date, that it verily seemed to turn up its nose to the traveller. I am sure it had a bathroom without a bathtub and various similar modern inconveniences. The barn was of the Agricultural-College type—it may be good, scientific, and all that, but it seems to crush everything else around out of existence; and it surely is not picturesque—unless it has wings and silos to relieve its rigid contours. Here it had not.

The other two farms to which I presently came—buildings set back from the road, but not so far as to give them the air of aloofness—had again that friendly, old-country expression that I have already mentioned: here it was somewhat marred, though, by an over-rigidity of the lines. It is unfortunate that our farmers, when they plant at all, will nearly always plant in straight lines. The straight line is a flaw where we try to blend the work of our hands with Nature. They also as a rule neglect shrubs that would help to furnish a foreground for their trees; and, worst of all, they are given to importing, instead of utilizing our native forest growth. Not often have I seen, for instance, our high-bush cranberry planted, although it certainly is one of the most beautiful shrubs to grow in copses.

These two farms proved to be pretty much the last

sign of comfort that I was to meet on my drives to the north. Though later I learned the names of their owners and even made their acquaintance, for me they remained the "half-way farms," for, after I had passed them, at the very next corner, I was seventeen miles from my starting point, seventeen miles from "home."

Beyond, stretches of the real wilderness began, the pioneer country, where farms, except along occasional highroads, were still three, four miles apart, where the breaking on few homesteads had reached the thirty-acre mark, and where a real, "honest-to-goodness" cash dollar bill was often as scarce as a well-to-do teacher in the prairie country.

The sun went down, a ball of molten gold—two hours from "town," as I called it. There were no rosy-fingered clouds; just a paling of the blue into white; then a greying of the western sky; and lastly the blue again, only this time dark. A friendly crescent still showed trail and landmarks after even the dusk had died away. Four miles, or a little more, and I should be in familiar land again. Four miles, that I longed to make, before the last light failed. . . .

The road angled to the northeast. I was by no means very sure of it. I knew which general direction to hold, but trails that often became mere cattle-paths crossed and criss-crossed repeatedly. It was too dark by this time to see very far. I did not know the small landmarks. But I knew, if I drove my horse pretty briskly, I must within little more than half an hour strike a black wall of the densest primeval forest fringing a creek—and, skirting this creek, I must find an old, weather-beaten lumber bridge. When I had crossed that bridge, I should know the landmarks again.

Underbrush everywhere, mostly symphoricarpus, I thought. Large trunks loomed up, charred with forest fires; here and there a round, white or light-grey stone, ghostly in the waning light, knee-high, I should judge. Once I passed the skeleton of a stable—the remnant of the buildings put up by a pioneer settler who had to give in after having wasted effort and substance and worn his knuckles to the bones. The wilderness uses human material up. . . .

A breeze from the north sprang up, and it turned strangely chilly. I started to talk to Peter, the loneliness seemed so oppressive. I told him that he should have a walk, a real walk, as soon as we had crossed the creek. I told him we were on the homeward half—that I had a bag of oats in the box, and that my wife would have a pail of water ready. . . . And Peter trotted along.

Something loomed up in front. Dark and sinister it looked. Still there was enough light to recognize even that which I did not know. A large bluff of poplars rustled, the wind soughing through the stems with a wailing note. The brush grew higher to the right. I suddenly noticed that I was driving along a broken-down fence between the brush and myself. The brush became a grove of boles which next seemed to shoot up to the full height of the bluff. Then, unexpectedly, startlingly, a vista opened. Between the silent grove to the south and the large, whispering, wailing bluff to the north there stood in a little clearing a snow-white log house, uncannily white in the paling moonlight. I could still distinctly see that its upper windows were nailed shut with boards— and yes, its lower ones, too. And yet, the moment I passed it, I saw, through one unclosed window on the north side, light. Unreasonably I shuddered.

This house, too, became a much-looked-for landmark to me on my future drives. I learned that it stood on the range line and called it the "White Range Line House." There hangs a story by this house. Maybe I shall one day tell it. . . .

Beyond the great and awe-inspiring poplar-bluff the

trail took a sharp turn eastward. From the southwest another rut-road joined it at the bend. I could only just make it out in the dark, for even moonlight was fading fast now. The sudden, reverberating tramp of the horse's feet betrayed that I was crossing a culvert. I had been absorbed in getting my bearings, and so it came as a surprise. It had not been mentioned in the elaborate directions which I had received with regard to the road to follow. For a moment, therefore, I thought I must be on the wrong trail. But just then the dim view, which had been obstructed by copses and thickets, cleared ahead in the last glimmer of the moon, and I made out the black cliff of forest darkly looming in the north—that forest I knew. Behind a narrow ribbon of bush the ground sloped down to the bed of the creek—a creek that filled in spring and became a torrent, but now was sluggish and slow where it ran at all. In places it consisted of nothing but a line of muddy pools strung along the bottom of its bed. In summer these were a favourite haunting place for mosquito-and-fly-plagued cows. There the great beasts would lie down in the mud and placidly cool their punctured skins. A few miles southwest the creek petered out entirely in a bed of shaly gravel bordering on the Big Marsh which I had skirted in my drive and a corner of which I was crossing just now.

The road was better here and spoke of more traffic. It was used to haul cordwood in late winter and early spring to a town some ten or fifteen miles to the southwest. So I felt sure again I was not lost but would presently emerge on familiar territory. The horse seemed to know it, too, for he raised his head and went at a better gait.

A few minutes passed. There was hardly a sound from my vehicle. The buggy was rubber-tired, and the horse selected a smooth ribbon of grass to run on. But from the black forest wall there came the soughing of the wind and the nocturnal rustle of things unknown. And suddenly there came from close at hand a startling sound: a clarion call that tore the veil lying over my mental vision: the sharp, repeated whistle of the whip-poor-will. And with my mind's eye I saw the dusky bird: shooting slantways upwards in its low flight which ends in a nearly perpendicular slide down to within ten or twelve feet from the ground, the bird being closely followed by a second one pursuing. In reality I did not see the birds, but I heard the fast whir of their wings.

Another bird I saw but did not hear. It was a small owl. The owl's flight is too silent, its wing is down-padded. You may hear its beautiful call, but you will not hear its flight, even though it circle right around your head in the dusk. This owl crossed my path not more than an inch or two in front. It nearly grazed my fore-head, so that I blinked. Oh, how I felt reassured! I believe, tears welled in my eyes. When I come to the home of frog and toad, of gartersnake and owl and whip-poor-will, a great tenderness takes possession of me, and I should like to shield and help them all and tell them not to be afraid of me; but I rather think they know it anyway.

The road swung north, and then east again; we skirted the woods; we came to the bridge; it turned straight north; the horse fell into a walk. I felt that henceforth I could rely on my sense of orientation to find the road. It was pitch dark in the bush—the thin slice of the moon had reached the horizon and followed the sun; no light struck into the hollow which I had to thread after turning to the southeast for a while. But as if to reassure me once more and still further of the absolute friendliness of all creation for myself—at this very moment I saw high overhead, on a dead branch of poplar, a snow-white owl, a large one, eighteen inches tall, sitting there in state, lord as he is of the realm of night. . . .

Peter walked—though I did not see the road, the horse could not mistake it. It lay at the bottom of a chasm of trees and bushes. I drew my cloak somewhat closer around and settled back. This cordwood trail took us on for half a mile, and then we came to a grade leading east. The grade was rough; it was the first one of a network of grades which were being built by the province, not primarily for the roads they afforded, but for the sake of the ditches of a bold and much needed drainage-system. To this very day these yellow grades of the pioneer country along the lake lie like naked scars on Nature's body: ugly, raw, as if the bowels were torn out of a beautiful bird and left to dry and rot on its plumage. Age will mellow them down into harmony.

Peter had walked for nearly half an hour. The ditch was north of the grade. I had passed, without seeing it, a newly cut-out road to the north which led to a lonesome schoolhouse in the bush. As always when I passed or thought of it, I had wondered where through this wilderness-tangle of bush and brush the children came from to fill it—walking through winter snows, through summer muds, for two, three, four miles or more to get their meagre share of the accumulated knowledge of the world. And the teacher! Was it the money? Could it be when there were plenty of schools in the thickly settled districts waiting for them? I knew of one who had come to this very school in a car and turned right back when she saw that she was expected to live as a boarder on a comfortless homestead and walk quite a distance and teach mostly foreign-born children. It had been the money with her! Unfortunately it is not the woman— nor the man either, for that matter—who drives around in a car, that will buckle down and do this nation's work! I also knew there were others like myself who

think this backwoods bushland God's own earth and
second only to Paradise—but few! And these young
girls that quake at their loneliness and yet go for a pit-
tance and fill a mission! But was not my wife of their
very number?

I started up. Peter was walking along. But here,
somewhere, there led a trail off the grade, down through
the ditch, and to the northeast into the bush which swal-
lows it up and closes behind it. This trail needs to be
looked for even in daytime, and I was to find it at night!
But by this time starlight began to aid. Vega stood nearly
straight overhead, and Deneb and Altair, the great
autumnal triangle in our skies. The Bear, too, stood out
boldly, and Cassiopeia opposite.

I drew in and got out of the buggy; and walking up
to the horse's head, got a hold of the bridle and led him,
meanwhile scrutinizing the ground over which I stepped.
At that I came near missing the trail. It was just a dark-
ening of the ground, a suggestion of black on the brown
of the grade, at the point where poles and logs had been
pulled across with the logging chain. I sprang down into
the ditch and climbed up beyond and felt with my foot
for the dent worn into the edge of the slope, to make
sure that I was where I should be. It was right, so I led
the horse across. At once he stood on three legs again,
left hindleg drawn up, and rested.

"Well, Peter," I said, "I suppose I have made it easy
enough for you. We have another twelve miles to make.
You'll have to get up." But Peter this time did not stir
till I touched him a flick with my whip.

The trail winds around, for it is a logging trail, leading up to the best bluffs, which are ruthlessly cut down
by the fuel-hunters. Only dead and half-decayed trees
are spared. But still young boles spring up in astonishing numbers. Aspen and balm predominate, though
there is some ash and oak left here and there, with a

conifer as the rarest treat for the lover of trees. It is a
pitiful thing to see a nation's heritage go into the dis-
card. In France or in England it would be tended as
something infinitely precious! The face of our country
as yet shows the youth of infancy, but we make it pre-
maturely old. The settler who should regard the trees as
his greatest pride, to be cut into as sparingly as is com-
patible with the exigencies of his struggle for life—he
regards them as a nuisance to be burned down by setting
wholesale fires to them. Already there is a scarcity of
fuel-wood in these parts.

Where the fires as yet have not penetrated too badly,
the cutting, which leaves only what is worthless, deter-
mines the impression the forest makes. At night this impression is distinctly uncanny. Like gigantic brooms
with their handles stuck into the ground, the dead wood
stands up; the underbrush crowds against it, so dense
that it lies like huge black cushions under the stars. The
inner recesses form an almost impenetrable mass of
young boles of shivering aspen and scented balm. This
mass slopes down to thickets of alder, red dogwood, haw,
high-bush cranberry, and honeysuckle, with wide beds
of goldenrod or purple asters shading off into the
spangled meadows wherever the copses open up into
grassy glades.

Through this bush, and skirting its meadows, I drove
for an hour. There was another fork in the trail, and
again I had to get out and walk on the side, to feel with
my foot for the rut where it branched to the north. And
then, after a while, the landscape opened up, the brush
receded. At last I became conscious of a succession of
posts to the right, and a few minutes later I emerged on
the second east-west grade. Another mile to the east
along this grade, and I should come to the last, homeward stretch.

Again I began to talk to the horse. "Only five miles

now, Peter, and then the night's rest. A good drink, a good feed of oats and wild hay, and the birds will waken you in the morning."

The northern lights leaped into the sky just as I turned from this east-west grade, north again, across a high bridge, to the last road that led home. To the right I saw a friendly light, and a dog's barking voice rang over from the still, distant farmstead. I knew the place. An American settler with a French-sounding name had squatted down there a few years ago.

The road I followed was, properly speaking, not a road at all, though used for one. A deep master ditch had been cut from ten or twelve miles north of here; it angled, for engineering reasons, so that I was going northwest again. The ground removed from the ditch had been dumped along its east side, and though it formed only a narrow, high, and steep dam, rough with stones and overgrown with weeds, it was used by whoever had to go north or south here. The next east-west grade which I was aiming to reach, four miles north, was the second correction line that I had to use, twenty-four miles distant from the first; and only a few hundred yards from its corner I should be at home!

At home! All my thoughts were bent on getting home now. Five or six hours of driving will make the strongest back tired, I am told. Mine is not of the strongest. This road lifted me above the things that I liked to watch. Invariably, on all these drives, I was to lose interest here unless the stars were particularly bright and brilliant. This night I watched the lights, it is true: how they streamed across the sky, like driving rain that is blown into wavy streaks by impetuous wind. And they leaped and receded, and leaped and receded again. But while I watched, I stretched my limbs and was bent on speed. There were a few particularly bad spots in the road, where I could not do anything but walk the horse. So,

where the going was fair, I urged him to redoubled effort.
I remember how I reflected that the horse as yet did not
know we were so near home, this being his first trip out;
and I also remember, that my wife afterwards told me
that she had heard me a long while before I came—had
heard me talking to the horse, urging him on and en-
couraging him.

Now I came to a slight bend in the road. Only half a
mile! And sure enough: there was the signal put out
for me. A lamp in one of the windows of the school—
placed so that after I turned in on the yard, I could not
see it—it might have blinded my eye, and the going is
rough there with stumps and stones. I could not see the
cottage, it stood behind the school. But the school I saw
clearly outlined against the dark blue, star-spangled sky,
for it stands on a high gravel ridge. And in the most
friendly and welcoming way it looked with its single eye
across at the nocturnal guest.

I could not see the cottage, but I knew that my little
girl lay sleeping in her cosy bed, and that a young
woman was sitting there in the dark, her face glued to
the window-pane, to be ready with a lantern which
burned in the kitchen whenever I might pull up between
school and house. And there, no doubt, she had been
sitting for a long while already; and there she was destined to sit during the winter that came, on Friday nights
—full often for many and many an hour—full often till
midnight—and sometimes longer.

Chapter 2

FOG

PETER took me north, alone, on six successive trips. We had rain, we had snow, we had mud and hard-frozen ground. It took us four, it took us six, it took us on one occasion—after a heavy October snowfall—nearly eleven hours to make the trip. That last adventure decided me. It was unavoidable that I should buy a second horse. The roads were getting too heavy for single driving over such a distance. This time I wanted a horse that I could sell in the spring to a farmer for any kind of work on the land. I looked around for a while. Then I found Dan. He was a sorrel, with some Clyde blood in him. He looked a veritable skate of a horse. You could lay your fingers between his ribs, and he played out on the first trip I ever made with this newly-assembled, strange-looking team. But when I look back at that winter, I cannot but say that again I chose well. After I had fed him up, he did the work in a thoroughly satisfactory manner, and he learnt to know the road far better than Peter. Several times I should have been lost without his unerring road sense. In the spring I sold him for exactly what I had paid; the farmer who bought him has him to this very day * and says he never had a better horse.

I also had found that on moonless nights it was indispensable for me to have lights along. Now maybe the reader has already noticed that I am rather a thoroughgoing person. For a week I worked every day after four at my buggy and finally had a blacksmith put on the finishing touches. What I rigged up, was as follows: On

* Spring, 1919.

the front springs I fastened with clamps two upright iron supports; between them with thumbscrews the search-light of a wrecked steam tractor which I got for a "Thank-you" from a junk-pile. Into the buggy box I laid a borrowed acetylene gas tank, strapped down with two bands of galvanized tin. I made the connection by a stout rubber tube, "guaranteed not to harden in the severest weather." To the side of the box I attached a short piece of band-iron, bent at an angle, so that a bicycle lamp could be slipped over it. Against the case that I should need a handlight, I carried besides a so-called dashboard coal-oil lantern with me. With all lamps going, it must have been a strange outfit to look at from a distance in the dark.

I travelled by this time in fur coat and cap, and I carried a robe for myself and blankets for the horses, for I now fed them on the road soon after crossing the creek.

Now on the second Friday of November there had been a smell of smoke in the air from the early morning. The marsh up north was afire—as it had been off and on for a matter of twenty-odd years. The fire consumes on the surface everything that will burn; the ground cools down, a new vegetation springs up, and nobody would suspect—as there is nothing to indicate—that only a few feet below the heat lingers, ready to leap up again if given the opportunity. In this case I was told that a man had started to dig a well on a newly-filed claim, and that suddenly he found himself wrapped about in smoke and flames. I cannot vouch for the truth of this, but I can vouch for the fact that the smoke of the fire was smelt for forty miles north and that in the afternoon a com-bination of this smoke (probably furnishing "condensa-tion nuclei") and of the moisture in the air, somewhere along or above the lake, brought about the densest fog I had ever seen on the prairies. How it spread, I shall dis-cuss later on. To give an idea of its density I will mention right here that on the well travelled road between two important towns a man abandoned his car during the early part of the night because he lost his nerve when his lights could no longer penetrate the fog sufficiently to reach the road.

I was warned at noon. "You surely do not intend to go out to-night?" remarked a lawyer-acquaintance to me at the dinner-table in the hotel; for by telephone from lake-points reports of the fog had already reached the town. "I intend to leave word at the stable right now," I replied, "to have team and buggy in front of the school at four o'clock." "Well," said the lawyer in getting up, "I would not; you'll run into fog."

And into fog I did run. At this time of the year I had at best only a little over an hour's start in my race against darkness. I always drove my horses hard now while day-light lasted; I demanded from them their very best strength at the start. Then, till we reached the last clear road over the dam, I spared them as much as I could. I had met up with a few things in the dark by now, and I had learned, if a difficulty arose, how much easier it is to cope with it even in failing twilight than by the gleam of lantern or headlight; for the latter never illumine more than a limited spot.

So I had turned Bell's corner by the time I hit the fog. I saw it in front and to the right. It drew a slanting line across the road. There it stood like a wall. Not a breath seemed to be stirring. The fog, from a distance, appeared to rise like a cliff, quite smoothly, and it blotted out the world beyond. When I approached it, I saw that its face was not so smooth as it had appeared from half a mile back; nor was it motionless. In fact, it was rolling south and west like a wave of great viscosity. Though my senses failed to perceive the slightest breath of a breeze, the fog was brewing and whirling, and huge spheres seemed to be forming in it, and to roll forward,

slowly, and sometimes to recede, as if they had encountered an obstacle and rebounded clumsily. I had
seen a tidal wave, fifty or more feet high, sweep up the
"bore" of a river at the head of the Bay of Fundy. I was
reminded of the sight; but here everything seemed to
proceed in a strangely, weirdly leisurely way. There was
none of that rush, of that hurry about this fog that
characterizes water. Besides there seemed to be no end
to the wave above; it reached up as far as your eye could
see—now bulging in, now out, but always advancing.
It was not so slow, however, as for the moment I judged
it to be; for I was later on told that it reached the town
at about six o'clock. And here I was, at five, six and a
half miles from its limits as the crow flies.

  I had hardly time to take in the details that I have
described before I was enveloped in the folds of the fog.
I mean this quite literally, for I am firmly convinced that
an onlooker from behind would have seen the grey
masses fold in like a sheet when I drove against them. It
must have looked as if a driver were driving against a
canvas moving in a slight breeze—canvas light and loose
enough to be held in place by the resistance of the air so
as to enclose him. Or maybe I should say "veiling" instead of canvas—or something still lighter and airier.
Have you ever seen milk poured carefully down the side
of a glass vessel filled with water? Well, clear air and
fog seemed to behave towards each other pretty much
the same way as milk in that case behaves towards water.

  I am rather emphatic about this because I have made
a study of just such mists on a very much smaller scale.
In that northern country where my wife taught her
school and where I was to live for nearly two years as a
convalescent, the hollows of the ground on clear cold
summer nights, when the mercury dipped down close to
the freezing point, would sometimes fill with a white
mist of extraordinary density. Occasionally this mist

would go on forming in higher and higher layers by condensation; mostly, however, it seemed rather to come from below. But always, when it was really dense, there was a definite plane of demarcation. In fact, that was the criterion by which I recognized this peculiar mist. Mostly there is, even in the north, a layer of lesser density over the pools, gradually shading off into the clear air above. Nothing of what I am going to describe can be observed in that case.

One summer, when I was living not over two miles from the lakeshore, I used to go down to these pools whenever they formed in the right way; and when I approached them slowly and carefully, I could dip my hand into the mist as into water, and I could feel the coolness of the misty layers. It was not because my hand got moist, for it did not. No evaporation was going on there, nor any condensation either. Nor did noticeable bubbles form because there was no motion in the mass which might have caused the infinitesimal droplets to collide and to coalesce into something perceivable to my senses.

Once, of a full-moon night, I spent an hour getting into a pool like that, and when I looked down at my feet, I could not see them. But after I had been standing in it for a while, ten minutes maybe, a clear space had formed around my body, and I could see the ground. The heat of my body helped the air to redissolve the mist into steam. And as I watched, I noticed that a current was set up. The mist was continually flowing in towards my feet and legs where the body-heat was least. And where evaporation proceeded fastest, that is at the height of my waist, little wisps of mist would detach themselves from the side of the funnel of clear air in which I stood, and they would, in a slow, graceful motion, accelerated somewhat towards the last, describe a downward and inward curve towards the lower part of my body before

they dissolved. I thought of that elusive and yet clearly
defined layer of mist that forms in the plane of contact
between the cold air flowing from Mammoth Cave in
Kentucky and the ambient air of a sultry summer day.*

On another of the rare occasions when the mists had
formed in the necessary density I went out again, put a
stone in my pocket and took a dog along. I approached
a shallow mist pool with the greatest caution. The dog
crouched low, apparently thinking that I was stalking
some game. Then, when I had arrived within about ten
or fifteen yards from the edge of the pool, I took the
stone from my pocket, showed it to the dog, and threw it
across the pool as fast and as far as I could. The dog
dashed in and tore through the sheet. Where the impact
of his body came, the mist bulged in, then broke. For a
while there were two sheets, separated by a more or less
clearly defined, vertical layer of transparency or maybe
blackness rather. The two sheets were in violent commotion, approaching, impinging upon each other, swinging back again to complete separation, and so on. But
the violence of the motion consisted by no means in
speed: it suggested a very much retarded rolling off of a
motion-picture reel. There was at first an element of dis-
illusion in the impression. I felt tempted to shout and to
spur the mist into greater activity. On the surface, to
both sides of the tear, waves ran out, and at the edges of
the pool they rose in that same leisurely, stately way
which struck me as one of the most characteristic
features of that November mist; and at last it seemed as
if they reared and reached up, very slowly, as a dying
man may stand up once more before he falls. And only
after an interval that seemed unconscionably long to me
the whole pool settled back to comparative smoothness,
though without its definite plane of demarcation now.

* See Burroughs' wonderful description of this phenomenon
in *Riverby*.

Strange to say, the dog had actually started something, a rabbit maybe or a jumping deer, and did not return.

When fogs spread, as a rule they do so in air already saturated with moisture. What really spreads, is the cold air which by mixing with, and thereby cooling, the warmer, moisture-laden atmosphere causes the condensation. That is why our fall mists mostly are formed in an exceedingly slight but still noticeable breeze. But in the case of these northern mist pools, whenever the conditions are favourable for their formation, the moisture of the upper air seems to be pretty well condensed as dew. It is only in the hollows of the ground that it remains suspended in this curious way. I cannot, so far, say whether it is due to the fact that where radiation is largely thrown back upon the walls of the hollow, the fall in temperature at first is very much slower than in the open, thus enabling the moisture to remain in suspension; or whether the hollows serve as collecting reservoirs for the cold air from the surrounding territory—the air carrying the already condensed moisture with it; or whether, lastly, it is simply due to a greater saturation of the atmosphere in these cavities, consequent upon the greater approach of their bottom to the level of the ground water. I have seen a "waterfall" of this mist overflow from a dent in the edge of ground that contained a pool. That seems to argue for an origin similar to that of a spring; as if strongly moisture-laden air welled up from underground, condensing its steam as it got chilled. It is these strange phenomena that are familiar, too, in the northern plains of Europe which must have given rise to the belief in elves and other weird creations of the brain —"the earth has bubbles as the water has"—not half as weird, though, as some realities are in the land which I love.

Now this great, memorable fog of that November Friday shared the nature of the mist pools of the north in as much as to a certain extent it refused to mingle with the drier and slightly warmer air into which it travelled. It was different from them in as much as it fairly dripped and oozed with a very palpable wetness. Just how it displaced the air in its path, is something which I cannot with certainty say. Was it formed as a low layer somewhere over the lake and slowly pushed along by a gentle, imperceptible, fan-shaped current of air? Fan-shaped, I say; for, as we shall see, it travelled simultaneously south and north; and I must infer that in exactly the same way it travelled west. Or was it formed originally like a tremendous column which flattened out by and by, through its own greater gravity slowly displacing the lighter air in the lower strata? I do not know, but I am inclined to accept the latter explanation. I do know that it travelled at the rate of about six miles an hour; and its coming was observed somewhat in detail by two other observers besides myself—two people who lived twenty-five miles apart, one to the north, one to the south of where I hit it. Neither one was as much interested in things meteorological as I am, but both were struck by the unusual density of the fog, and while one saw it coming from the north, the other one saw it approaching from the south.

I have no doubt that at last it began to mingle with the clearer air and to thin out; in fact, I have good testimony to that effect. And early next morning it was blown by a wind like an ordinary fog-cloud all over Portage Plains.

I also know that further north, at my home, for instance, it had the smell of the smoke which could not have proceeded from anywhere but the marsh; and the marsh lay to the south of it. That seemed to prove that actually the mist was spreading from a common centre in at least two directions. These points, which I gathered later, strongly confirmed my own observations, which

will be set down further on. It must, then, have been
formed as a layer of a very considerable height, to be
able to spread over so many square miles.

As I said, I was reminded of those mist pools in the
north when I approached the cliff of the fog, especially
of that "waterfall" of mist of which I spoke. But besides
the difference in composition—the fog, as we shall see,
was not homogeneous, this being the cause of its wetness
—there was another important point of distinction. For,
while the mist of the pools is of the whitest white, this
fog showed from the outside and in the mass—the single
wreaths seemed white enough—rather the colour of that
"wet, unbleached linen" of which Burroughs speaks in
connection with rain-clouds.

Now, as soon as I was well engulfed in the fog, I had
a few surprises. I could no longer see the road ahead; I
could not see the fence along which I had been driving;
I saw the horses' rumps, but I did not see their heads. I
bent forward over the dashboard: I could not even see
the ground below. It was a series of negatives. I stopped
the horses. I listened—then looked at my watch. The
stillness of the grave enveloped me. It was a little past
five o'clock. The silence was oppressive—the misty im-
penetrability of the atmosphere was appalling. I do not
say "darkness," for as yet it was not really dark. I could
still see the dial of my watch clearly enough to read the
time. But darkness was falling fast—"falling," for it
seemed to come from above: mostly it rises—from out
of the shadows under the trees—advancing, fighting
back the powers of light above.

One of the horses, I think it was Peter, coughed. It
was plain they felt chilly. I thought of my lights and
started with stiffening fingers to fumble at the valves of
my gas tank. When reaching into my trouser pockets for
matches, I was struck with the astonishing degree to
which my furs had been soaked in these few minutes. As

for wetness, the fog was like a sponge. At last, kneeling
in the buggy box, I got things ready. I smelt the gas es-
caping from the burner of my bicycle lantern and heard
it hissing in the headlight. The problem arose of how to
light a match. I tried various places—without success.
Even the seat of my trousers proved disappointing. I got
a sizzling and sputtering flame, it is true, but it went out
before I could apply it to the gas. The water began to
drip from the backs of my hands. It was no rain because
it did not fall. It merely floated along; but the droplets,
though smaller, were infinitely more numerous than in a
rain—there were more of them in a given space. At last
I lifted the seat cushion under which I had a tool box
filled with ropes, leather straps and all manner of things
that I might ever be in need of during my nights in the
open. There I found a dry spot where to strike the needed
match. I got the bicycle lantern started. It burned quite
well, and I rather admired it: unreasonably I seemed
to have expected that it would not burn in so strange an
atmosphere. So I carefully rolled a sheet of letter paper
into a fairly tight roll, working with my back to the fog
and under the shelter of my big raccoon coat. I took a
flame from the bicycle light and sheltered and nursed it
along till I thought it would stand the drizzle. Then I
turned and thrust the improvised torch into the bulky
reflector case of the searchlight. The result was startling.
A flame eighteen inches high leaped up with a crackling
and hissing sound.

The horses bolted, and the buggy jumped. I was
lucky, for inertia carried me right back on the seat, and
as soon as I had the lines in my hands again, I felt that
the horses did not really mean it. I do not think we had
gone more than two or three hundred yards before the
team was under control. I stopped and adjusted the over-
turned valves. When I succeeded, I found to my disappointment that the heat of that first flame had partly

spoiled the reflector. Still, my range of vision now extended to the belly-band in the horses' harness. The light that used to show me the road for about fifty feet in front of the horses' heads gave a short truncated cone of great luminosity, which was interesting and looked reassuring; but it failed to reach the ground, for it was so adjusted that the focus of the converging light rays lay ahead and not below. Before, therefore, the point of greatest luminosity was reached, the light was completely absorbed by the fog.

I got out of the buggy, went to the horses' heads and patted their noses which were dripping with wetness. But now that I faced the headlight, I could see it though I had failed to see the horses' heads when seated behind it. This, too, was quite reassuring, for it meant that the horses probably could see the ground even though I did not.

But where was I? I soon found out that we had shot off the trail. And to which side? I looked at my watch again. Already the incident had cost me half an hour. It was really dark by now, even outside the fog, for there was no moon. I tried out how far I could get away from the buggy without losing sight of the light. It was only a very few steps, not more than a dozen. I tried to visualize where I had been when I struck the fog. And fortunately my habit of observing the smallest details, even if only subconsciously, helped me out. I concluded that the horses had bolted straight ahead, thus missing an S-shaped curve to the right.

At this moment I heard Peter paw the ground impatiently; so I quickly returned to the horses, for I did not relish the idea of being left alone. There was an air of impatience and nervousness about both of them.

I took my bicycle lantern and reached for the lines. Then, standing clear of the buggy, I turned the horses at right angles, to the north, as I imagined it to be. When we started, I walked alongside the team through dripping underbrush and held the lantern with my free hand close down to the ground.

Two or three times I stopped during the next half hour, trying, since we still did not strike the trail, to reason out a different course. I was now wet through and through up to my knees; and I had repeatedly run into willow clumps, which did not tend to make me any drier either. At last I became convinced that in bolting the horses must have swerved a little to the south, so that in starting up again we had struck a tangent to the big bend north, just beyond Bell's farm. If that was the case, we should have to make another turn to the right in order to strike the road again, for at best we were then simply going parallel to it. The trouble was that I had nothing to tell me the directions, not even a tree the bark or moss of which might have vouchsafed information. Suddenly I had an inspiration. Yes, the fog was coming from the northeast! So, by observing the drift of the droplets I could find at least an approximate meridian line. I went to the headlight, and an observation immediately confirmed my conjecture. I was now convinced that I was on that wild land where two months ago I had watched the goldfinches disporting themselves in the evening sun. But so as not to turn back to the south, I struck out at an angle of only about sixty degrees to my former direction. I tried not to swerve, which involved rough going, and I had many a stumble. Thus I walked for another half hour or thereabout.

Then, certainly! This was the road! The horses turned into it of their own accord. That was the most reassuring thing of all. There was one strange doubt left. Somehow I was not absolutely clear about it whether north might not after all be behind. I stopped. Even a new observation of the fog did not remove the last

vestige of a doubt. I had to take a chance, some landmark might help after a while.

I believe in getting ready before I start. So I took
my coal-oil lantern, lighted and suspended it under the
rear springs of the buggy in such a way that it would
throw its light back on the road. Having the light away
down, I expected to be able to see at least whether I was
on a road or not. In this I was only partly successful;
for on the rut-trails nothing showed except the blades of
grass and the tops of weeds; while on the grades where
indeed I could make out the ground, I did not need a
light, for, as I found out, I could more confidently rely on
my ear.

I got back to my seat and proceeded to make myself
as comfortable as I could. I took off my shoes and socks
—keeping well under the robe—extracted a pair of
heavy woollens from my suitcase under the seat, rubbed
my feet dry and then wrapped up, without putting my
shoes on again, as carefully and scientifically as only a
man who has had pneumonia and is a chronic sufferer
from pleuritis knows how to do.

At last I proceeded. After listening again with great
care for any sound I touched the horses with my whip,
and they fell into a quiet trot. It was nearly seven now,
and I had probably not yet made eight miles. We swung
along. If I was right in my calculations and the horses
kept to the road, I should strike the "twelve-mile bridge"
in about three-quarters of an hour. That was the bridge
leading through the cottonwood gate to the grade past
the "hovel." I kept the watch in the mitt of my left hand.

Not for a moment did it occur to me to turn back. Way
up north there was a young woman preparing supper for
me. The fog might not be there—she would expect me—
I could not disappoint her. And then there was the little
girl, who usually would wake up and in her "nightie"
come out of bed and sleepily smile at me and climb on

to my knee and nod off again. I thought of them, to be
sure, of the hours and hours in wait for them, and a great
tenderness came over me, and gratitude for the belated
home they gave an aging man. . . .

And slowly my mind reverted to the things at hand.
And this is what was the most striking feature about
them: I was shut in, closed off from the world around.
Apart from that cone of visibility in front of the headlight, and another much smaller one from the bicycle
lamp, there was not a thing I could see. If the road was
the right one, I was passing now through some square
miles of wild land. Right and left there were poplar
thickets, and ahead there was that line of stately cottonwoods. But no suggestion of a landmark—nothing except a cone of light which was filled with fog and cut
into on both sides by two steaming and rhythmically
moving horseflanks. It was like a very small room, this
space of light—the buggy itself, in darkness, forming an
alcove to it, in which my hand knew every well-ap-
pointed detail. Gradually, while I was warming up, a
sense of infinite comfort came, and with it the enjoyment
of the elvish aspect.

I began to watch the fog. By bending over towards
the dashboard and looking into the soon arrested glare
I could make out the component parts of the fog. It was
like the mixture of two immiscible liquids—oil, for instance, shaken up with water. A fine, impalpable, yet
very dense mist formed the ground mass. But in it there
floated myriads of droplets, like the droplets of oil in
water. These droplets would sometimes sparkle in a mild,
unobtrusive way as they were nearing the light; and then
they would dash against the pane and keep it dripping,
dripping down.

I leaned back again; and I watched the whole of the
light-cone. Snow-white wisps would float and whirl
through it in graceful curves, stirred into motion by the

horses' trot. Or a wreath of it would start to dance, as if gently pulled or plucked at from above; and it would revolve, faster towards the end, and fade again into the shadows behind. I thought of a summer in Norrland, in Sweden, in the stone-and-birch waste which forms the timberline, where I had also encountered the mist pools. And a trip down a stream in the borderland of the Finns came back with great vividness into my mind. That trip had been made in a fog like this; only it had been begun in the early morning, and the whole mass of the mist had been suffused with the whitest of lights. But strange to say, what stood out most strikingly in the fleeting memory of the voyage, was the weird and mocking laughter of the magpies all along the banks. The Finnish woods seemed alive with that mocking laughter, and it truly belongs to the land of the mists. For a moment I thought that something after all was missing here on the prairies. But then I reflected again that this silence of the grave was still more perfect, still more uncanny and ghostly, because it left the imagination entirely free, without limiting it by even as much as a suggestion.

No wonder, I thought, that the Northerners in their land of heath and bog were the poets of elves and goblins and of the fear of ghosts. Shrouds were these fogs, hanging and waving and floating shrouds! Mocking spirits were plucking at them and setting them into their gentle motions. Gleams of light, that dance over the bog, lured you in, and once caught in these veils after veils of mystery, madness would sieze you, and you would wildly dash here and there in a vain attempt at regaining your freedom; and when, exhausted at last, you broke down and huddled together on the ground, the werwolf would come, ghostly himself, and huge and airy and weird, his body woven of mist, and in the fog's stately and leisurely way he would kneel down on your chest, slowly crushing you beneath his exceeding weight; and bending and straightening, bending and stretching, slowly—slowly down came his head to your throat; and then he would lie and not stir until morning and suck; and after few or many days people would find you, dead in the woods—a victim of fog and mist. . . .

A rumbling sound made me sit up at last. We were crossing over the "twelve-mile bridge." In spite of my dreaming I was keeping my eyes on the look-out for any sign of a landmark, but this was the only one I had known so far, and it came through the ear, not the eye. I promptly looked back and up, to where the cotton-woods must be; but no sign of high, weeping trees, no rustling of fall-dry leaves, not even a deeper black in the black betrayed their presence. Well, never before had I failed to see some light, to hear some sound around the house of the "moneyed" type or those of the "half-way farms." Surely, somehow I should be aware of their presence when I got there! Some sign, some landmark would tell me how far I had gone! . . . The horses were trotting along, steaming, through the brewing fog. I had become all ear. Even though my buggy was silent and though the road was coated with a thin film of soft clay-mud, I could distinctly hear by the muffled thud of the horses' hoofs on the ground that they were running over a grade. That confirmed my bearings. I had no longer a moment's doubt or anxiety over my drive.

The grade was left behind, the rut-road started again, was passed and outrun. So now I was close to the three-farm cluster. I listened intently for the horses' thump. Yes, there was that muffled hoof-beat again—I was on the last grade that led to the angling road across the corner of the marsh.

Truly, this was very much like lying down in the sleeping-car of an overland train. You recline and act as if nothing unusual were going on; and meanwhile a force that has something irresistible about it and is indeed largely beyond your control, wafts you over mile after mile of fabled distance; now and then the rumble of car on rail will stop, the quiet awakens you, lights flash their piercing darts, a voice calls out; it is a well-known stop on your journey and then the rumbling resumes, you doze again, to be awakened again, and so on. And when you get up in the morning—there she lies, the goal of your dreams—the resplendent city. . . .

My goal was my "home," and, mildly startling, at least one such mid-nightly awakening came. I had kept peering about for a landmark, a light. Somewhere here in those farmhouses which I saw with my mind's eye, people were sitting around their fireside, chatting or reading. Lamps shed their homely light; roof and wall kept the fog-spook securely out: nothing as comfortable then as to listen to stories of being lost on the marsh, or to tell them. . . . But between those people and myself the curtain had fallen—no sign of their presence, no faintest gleam of their light and warmth! They did not know of the stranger passing outside, his whole being a-yearn with the desire for wife and child. I listened intently—no sound of man or beast, no soughing of wind in stems or rustling of the very last leaves that were now fast falling. . . . And then the startling neighing of Dan, my horse! This was the third trip he made with me, and I might have known and expected it, but it always came as a surprise. Whenever we passed that second farm, he stopped and, raising his head with a sideways motion, neighed a loud and piercing call. And now he had stopped and done it again. He knew where we were. I lowered my whip and patted his rump. How did he know? And why did he do it? Was there a horse on this farmstead which he had known in former life? Or was it a man? Or did he merely feel that it was about time to put in for the night? I enquired later on, but failed to discover any reason for his behaviour.

Now came that angling road past the "White Range Line House." I relied on the horses entirely. This "Range Line House" was inhabited now—a settler was putting in winter-residence so he might not lose his claim. He had taken down the clapboards that closed the windows, and always had I so far seen a light in the house.

It seemed to me that in this corner of the marsh the fog was less dense than it had been farther south, and the horses, once started, were swinging along, though in a leisurely way, yet without hesitation. Another half hour passed. Once, at a bend in the trail, the rays from the powerful tractor searchlight, sweeping sideways past the horses, struck a wetly glistening, greyish stone to the right of the road. I knew that stone. Yes, surely the fog must be thinning, or I could not have seen it. I could now also dimly make out the horses' heads, as they nodded up and down. . . .

And then, like a phantom, way up in the mist, I made out a blacker black in the black—the majestic poplars north of the "Range Line House." Not that I could really see them or pick out the slightest detail—no! But it seemed to my searching eyes as if there was a quiet pool in the slow flow of the fog—as the water in a slow-flowing stream will come to rest when it strikes the stems of a willow submerged at its margin. I was trying even at the time to decide how much of what I seemed to divine rather than to perceive was imagination and how much reality. And I was just about ready to contend that I also saw to the north something like the faintest possible suggestion of an eddy, such as would form in the flowing water below a pillar or a rock—when I was rudely shaken up and jolted.

Trap, trap, I heard the horses' feet on the culvert. Crash! And Peter went stumbling down. Then a violent lurch of the buggy, I holding on—Peter rallied, and then, before I had time to get a firmer grasp on the lines, both horses bolted again. It took me some time to realize what had happened. It was the culvert, of course; it had broken down, and lucky I was that the ditch underneath was shallow. Only much later, when reflecting upon the incident, did I see that this accident was really the best verification of what I was nearly inclined to regard as the product of my imagination. The trees must indeed have stood where I had seemed to see that quiet reach in the fog and that eddy....

We tore along. I spoke to the horses and quietly and evenly pulled at the lines. I think it must have been several minutes before I had them under control again. And then—in this night of weird things—the weirdest sight of them all showed ahead.

I was just beginning to wonder, whether after all we had not lost the road again, when the faintest of all faint glimmers began to define itself somewhere in front. And . . . was I right? Yes, a small, thin voice came out of the fog that incessantly floated into my cone of light and was left behind in eddies. What did it mean? . . .

The glimmer was now defining itself more clearly. Somewhere, not very far ahead and slightly to the left, a globe of the faintest iridescent luminosity seemed suspended in the brewing and waving mist. The horses turned at right angles on to the bridge, the glimmer swinging round to the other side of the buggy. Their hoofs struck wood, and both beasts snorted and stopped.

In a flash a thought came. I had just broken through a culvert—the bridge, too, must have broken down, and somebody had put a light there to warn the chance traveller who might stray along on a night like this! I was on the point of getting out of my wraps, when a thinner wave in the mist permitted me to see the flames of three lanterns hung to the side-rails of the bridge. And that very moment a thin, piping voice came out of

the darkness beyond. "Daddy, is that you?" I did not
know the child's voice, but I sang out as cheerily as I
could. "I am a daddy all right, but I am afraid, not yours.
Is the bridge broken down, sonny? Anything wrong?"
"No, Sir," the answer came, "nothing wrong." So
I pulled up to the lanterns, and there I saw, dimly
enough, God wot, a small ten-year-old boy standing and
shivering by the signal which he had rigged up. He was
barefooted and bareheaded, in shirt and torn knee-
trousers. I pointed to the lanterns with my whip. "What's
the meaning of this, my boy?" I asked in as friendly a
voice as I could muster. "Daddy went to town this morning," he said rather haltingly, "and he must have got
caught in the fog. We were afraid he might not find the
bridge." "Well, cheer up, son," I said, "he is not the only
one as you see; his horses will know the road. Where did
he go?" The boy named the town—it was to the west,
not half the distance away that I had come. "Don't
worry," I said; "I don't think he has started out at all.
The fog caught me about sixteen miles south of here. It's
nine o'clock now. If he had started before the fog got
there, he would be here by now." I sat and thought for a
moment. Should I say anything about the broken culvert? "Which way would your daddy come, along the
creek or across the marsh?" "Along the creek." All right
then, no use in saying anything further. "Well, as I said,"
I sang out and clicked my tongue to the horses, "don't
worry; better go home; he will come to-morrow." "I
guess so," replied the boy the moment I lost sight of him
and the lanterns.

I made the turn to the southeast and walked my
horses. Here, where the trail wound along through the
chasm of the bush, the light from my cone would, over
the horses' backs, strike twigs and leaves now and then.
Everything seemed to drip and to weep. All nature was
weeping. I walked the horses for ten minutes more.

Then I stopped. It must have been just at the point where the grade began; but I do not know for sure.

I fumbled a long while for my shoes; but at last I found them and put them on over my dry woollens. When I had shaken myself out of my robes, I jumped to the ground. There was, here, too, a film of mud on top, but otherwise the road was firm enough. I quickly threw the blankets over the horses' backs, dropped the traces, took the bits out of their mouths, and slipped the feed-bags over their heads. I looked at my watch, for it was my custom to let them eat for just ten minutes, then to hook them up again and walk them for another ten before trotting. I had found that that refreshed them enough to make the remainder of the trip in excellent shape.

While I was waiting, I stood between the wheels of the buggy, leaning against the box and staring into the light. It was with something akin to a start that I realized the direction from which the fog rolled by: it came from the south! I had, of course, seen that already, but it had so far not entered my consciousness as a definite observation. It was this fact that later set me to thinking about the origin of the fog along the lines which I have indicated above. Again I marvelled at the density of the mist which somehow seemed greater while we were standing than while we were driving. I had repeatedly been in the clouds, on mountainsides, but they seemed light and thin as compared with this. Finland, Northern Sweden, Canada—no other country which I knew had anything resembling it. The famous London fogs are different altogether. These mists, like the mist pools, need the swamp as their mother, I suppose, and the ice-cool summer night for their nurse. . . .

The time was up. I quickly did what had to be done, and five minutes later we were on the road again. I watched the horses for a while, and suddenly I thought once more of that fleeting impression of an eddy in the lee of the poplar bluff at the "White Range Line House." It was on the north side of the trees, if it was there at all! The significance of the fact had escaped me at the time. It again confirmed my observation of the flow of the fog in both directions. It came from a common centre. And still there was no breath of air. I had no doubt any longer; it was not the air that pushed the fog; the floating bubbles, the infinitesimally small ones as well as those that were quite perceptible, simply displaced the lighter atmosphere. I wondered what kept these bubbles apart. Some repellent force with which they were charged? Something, at any rate, must be preventing them from coalescing into rain. Maybe it was merely the perfect evenness of their flow, for they gathered thickly enough on the twigs and the few dried leaves, on any obstacles in their way. And again I thought of the fact that the mist had seemed thinner when I came out on the marsh. This double flow explained it, of course. There were denser and less dense waves in it; like veils hung up one behind the other. So long as I went in a direction opposite to its flow, I had to look through sheet after sheet of the denser waves. Later I could every now and then look along a plane of lesser density. . . .

It was Dan who found the turn off the grade into the bushy glades. I could see distinctly how he pushed Peter over. Here, where again the road was winding, and where the light, therefore, once more frequently struck the twigs and boughs, as they floated into my cone of luminosity, to disappear again behind, a new impression thrust itself upon me. I call it an impression, not an observation. It is very hard to say, what was reality, what fancy on a night like that. In spite of its air of unreality, of improbability even, it has stayed with me as one of my strongest visions. I nearly hesitate to put it in writing.

These boughs and twigs were like fingers held into a

stream that carried loose algae, arresting them in their gliding motion. Or again, those wisps of mist were like gossamers as they floated along, and they would bend and fold over on the boughs before they tore; and where they broke, they seemed like comets to trail a thinner tail of themselves behind. There was tenacity in them, a certain consistency which made them appear as if woven of different things from air and mere moisture. I have often doubted my memory here, and yet I have my very definite notes, and besides there is the picture in my mind. In spite of my own uncertainty I can assure you, that this is only one-quarter a poem woven of impressions; the other three-quarters are reality. But, while I am trying to set down facts, I am also trying to render moods and images begot by them. . . .

We went on for an hour, and it lengthened out into two. No twigs and boughs any longer, at last. But where I was, I knew not. Much as I listened, I could not make out any difference in the tramp of the horses now. I looked down over the back of my buggy seat, and I seemed to see the yellow or brownish clay of a grade. I went on rather thoughtlessly. Then, about eleven o'clock, I noticed that the road was rough. I had long since, as I said, given myself over to the horses. But now I grew nervous. No doubt, unless we had entirely strayed from our road, we were by this time riding the last dam; for no other trail over which we went was quite so rough. But then I should have heard the rumble on the bridge, and I felt convinced that I had not. It shows to what extent a man may be hypnotized into insensibility by a constant sameness of view, that I was mistaken. If we were on the dam and missed the turn at the end of it, on to the correction line, we should infallibly go down from the grade, on to muskeg ground, for there was a gap in the dam. At that place I had seen a horse disappear, and many a cow had ended there in the deadly struggle against the downward suck of the swamp. . . .

I pulled the horses back to a walk, and we went on for another half hour. I was by this time sitting on the left-hand side of the seat, bicycle lantern in my left hand, and bending over as far as I could to the left, trying, with arm outstretched, to reach the ground with my light. The lantern at the back of the buggy was useless for this. Here and there the drop-laden, glistening tops of the taller grasses and weeds would float into this auxiliary cone of light—but that was all.

Then no weeds appeared any longer, so I must be on the last half-mile of the dam, the only piece of it that was bare, and caution extreme was the word. I made up my mind to go on riding for another five minutes and timed myself, for there was hardly enough room for a team and a walking man besides. When the time was up, I pulled in and got out. I took the lines short, laid my right hand on Peter's back and proceeded. The bicycle lantern was hanging down from my left and showed plainly the clayey gravel of the dam. And so I walked on for maybe ten minutes.

Suddenly I became again aware of a glimmer to the left, and the very next moment a lantern shot out of the mist, held high by an arm wrapped in white. A shivering woman, tall, young, with gleaming eyes, dressed in a linen house dress, an apron flung over breast and shoulders, gasped out two words, "You came!" "Have you been standing here and waiting?" I asked. "No, no! I just could not bear it any longer. Something told me. He's at the culvert now, and if I do not run, he will go down into the swamp!" There was something of a catch in the voice. I did not reply. I swung the horses around and crossed the culvert that bridges the master ditch.

And while we were walking up to the yard—had my

drive been anything brave—anything at all deserving of the slightest reward—had it not in itself been a thing of beauty, not to be missed by selfish me—surely, the touch of that arm, as we went, would have been more than enough to reward even the most chivalrous deeds of yore.

Chapter 3

DAWN AND DIAMONDS

Two days before Christmas the ground was still bare. I had a splendid new cutter with a top and side curtains; a heavy outfit, but one that would stand up, I believed, under any road conditions. I was anxious to use it, too, for I intended to spend a two weeks' holiday up north with my family. I was afraid, if I used the buggy, I might find it impossible to get back to town, seeing that the first heavy winter storms usually set in about the turn of the year.

School had closed at noon. I intended to set out next morning at as early an hour as I could. I do not know what gave me my confidence, but I firmly expected to find snow on the ground by that time. I am rather a student of the weather. I worked till late at night getting my cutter ready. I had to adjust my buggy pole and to stow away a great number of parcels. The latter included the first real doll for my little girl, two or three picture books, a hand sleigh, Pip—a little stuffed dog of the silkiest fluffiness—and as many more trifles for wife and child as my Christmas allowance permitted me to buy. It was the first time in the five years of my married life that, thanks to my wife's co-operation in earning money, there was any Christmas allowance to spend; and since I am writing this chiefly for her and the little girl's future reading, I want to set it down here, too, that it was thanks to this very same co-operation that I had been able to buy the horses and the driving outfit which I needed badly, for the poor state of my health forbade more rigorous exercise. I have already said, I think, that I am essentially an outdoor creature; and for several

years the fact that I had been forced to look at the out-
of-doors from the window of a town house only, had
been eating away at my vitality. Those drives took de-
cades off my age, and in spite of incurable illness my few
friends say that I look once more like a young man.

Besides my Christmas parcels I had to take oats along,
enough to feed the horses for two weeks. And I was, as
I said, engaged that evening in stowing everything away,
when about nine o'clock one of the physicians of the
town came into the stable. He had had a call into the
country, I believe, and came to order a team. When he
saw me working in the shed, he stepped up and said,
"You'll kill your horses." "Meaning?" I queried. "I see
you are getting your cutter ready," he replied. "If I were
you, I should stick to the wheels." I laughed. "I might
not be able to get back to work." "Oh yes," he scoffed,
"it won't snow up before the end of next month. We
figure on keeping the cars going for a little while yet."
Again I laughed. "I hope not," I said, which may not
have sounded very gracious.

At ten o'clock every bolt had been tightened, the
horses' harness and their feed were ready against the
morning, and everything looked good to me.

I was going to have the first real Christmas again in
twenty-five years, with a real Christmas tree, and with
wife and child, and even though it was a poor man's
Christmas, I refused to let anything darken my Christmas spirit or dull the keen edge of my enjoyment. Before
going out, I stepped into the office of the stable, slipped
a half-dollar into the hostler's palm and asked him once
more to be sure to have the horses fed at half-past five
in the morning.

Then I left. A slight haze filled the air, not heavy
enough to blot out the stars, but sufficient to promise
hoarfrost at least. Somehow there was no reason to
despair as yet of Christmas weather.

I went home and to bed and slept about as soundly as I could wish. When the alarm of my clock went off at five in the morning, I jumped out of bed and hurried down to shake the fire into activity. As soon as I had started something of a blaze, I went to the window and looked out. It was pitch dark, of course, the moon being down by this time, but it seemed to me that there was snow on the ground. I lighted a lamp and held it to the window; and sure enough, its rays fell on white upon white on shrubs and fence posts and window ledge. I laughed and instantly was in a glow of impatience to be off.

At half past five, when the coffee water was in the kettle and on the stove, I hurried over to the stable across the bridge. The snow was three inches deep, enough to make the going easy for the horses. The slight haze persisted, and I saw no stars. At the stable I found, of course, that the horses had not been fed; so I gave them oats and hay and went to call the hostler. When after much knocking at last he responded to my impatience, he wore a guilty look on his face but assured me that he was just getting up to feed my team. "Never mind about feeding," I said. "I've done that. But have them harnessed and hitched up by a quarter past six. I'll water them on the road." They never drank their fill before nine o'clock. And I hurried home to get my breakfast. . . .

"Merry Christmas!" the hostler called after me; and I shouted back over my shoulder, "The same to you." The horses were going under the merry jingle of the bells which they carried for the first time this winter.

I rarely could hold them down to a walk or a trot now, since the cold weather had set in; and mostly, before they even had cleared the slide-doors, they were in a gallop. Peter had changed his nature since he had a mate. By feeding and breeding he was so much Dan's superior

in vitality that, into whatever mischief the two got themselves, he was the leader. For all times the picture, seen
by the light of a lantern, stands out in my mind how he
bit at Dan, wilfully, urging him playfully on, when we
swung out into the crisp, dark, hazy morning air. Dan
being nothing loth and always keen at the start, we shot
across the bridge.

It was hard now, mostly, to hitch them up. They
would leap and rear with impatience when taken into
the open before they were hooked to the vehicle. They
were being very well fed, and though once a week they
had the hardest of work, for the rest of the time they had
never more than enough to limber them up, for on
schooldays I used to take them out for a spin of three or
four miles only, after four. At home, when I left, my wife
and I would get them ready in the stable; then I took
them out and lined them up in front of the buggy. My
wife quickly took the lines: I hooked the traces up,
jumped in, grabbed for the lines and waved my last fare-
well from the road afar off. Even at that they got away
from us once or twice and came very near upsetting and
wrecking the buggy; but nothing serious ever happened
during the winter. I had to have horses like that, for I
needed their speed and their staying power, as the reader
will see if he cares to follow me very much farther.

We flew along—the road seemed ideal—the air was
wonderfully crisp and cold—my cutter fulfilled the
highest expectations—the horses revelled in speed. But
soon I pulled them down to a trot, for I followed the
horsemen's rules whenever I could, and Dan, as I mentioned, was anyway rather too keen at the start for steady
work later on. I settled back. The top of my cutter was
down, for not a breath stirred, and I was always anxious
to see as much of the country as I could. . . .

Do you know which is the stillest hour of the night?
The hour before dawn. It is at that time, too, that in our

winter nights the mercury dips down to its lowest level.
Perhaps the two things have a casual relation—whatever
there is of wild life in nature, withdraws more deeply
within itself; it curls up and dreams. On calm summer
mornings you hear no sound except the chirping and
twittering of the sleeping birds. The birds are great
dreamers—like dogs; like dogs they will twitch and stir
in their sleep, as if they were·running and flying and
playing and chasing each other. Just stalk a bird's nest of
which you know at half past two in the morning, some
time during the month of July; and before you see them,
you will hear them. If there are young birds in the nest,
all the better; take the mother bird off and the little ones
will open their beaks, all mouth as they are, and go to
sleep again; and they will stretch their featherless little
wings; and if they are a little bit older, they will even try
to move their tiny legs, as if longing to use them. As with
dogs, it is the young ones that dream most. I suppose
their impressions are so much more vivid, the whole
world is so new to them that it rushes in upon them
charged with emotion. Emotions penetrate even us to a
greater depth than mere apperceptions; so they break
through that crust that seems to envelop the seat of our
memory, and once inside, they will work out again into
some form of consciousness—that of sleep or of the
wakeful dream which we call memory.

The stillest hour! In starlit winter nights the heavenly
bodies seem to take on an additional splendour. something next to blazing, overweening boastfulness. "Now
sleeps the world," they seem to say, "but we are awake
and weaving destiny." And on they swing on their
immutable paths.

The stillest hour! If you step out of a sleeping house
and are alone, you are apt to hold your breath; and if
you are not, you are apt to whisper. There is an expect-
ancy in the air, a fatefulness—a loud word would be

blasphemy that offends the ear and the feeling of
decency. It is the hour of all still things, the silent things
that pass like dreams through the night. You seem to
stand hushed. Stark and bare, stripped of all accidentals,
the universe swings on its way.

The stillest hour! But how much stiller than still,
when the earth has drawn over its shoulders that morning mist that allows of no slightest breath—when under
the haze the very air seems to lie curled and to have gone
to sleep. And yet how portentous! The haze seems to
brood. It seems somehow to suggest that there is all of life
asleep on earth. You seem to feel rather than to hear the
whole creation breathing in its sleep—as if it was sound-
lessly stirring in dreams—presently to stretch, to awake.
There is also the delicacy, the tenderness of all young
things about it. Even in winter it reminds me of the very
first unfolding of young leaves on trees; of the few hours
while they are still hanging down, unable to raise themselves up as yet; they look so worldlywise sometimes, so
precocious, and before them there still lie all hopes and
all disappointments. . . . In clear nights you forget the
earth—under the hazy cover your eye is thrown back
upon it. It is the contrast of the universe and of creation.

We drove along—and slowly, slowly came the dawn.
You could not define how it came. The whole world
seemed to pale and to whiten, and that was all. There
was no sunrise. It merely seemed as if all of Nature—
very gradually—was soaking itself full of some light; it
was dim at first, but never grey; and then it became the
whitest, the clearest, the most undefinable light. There
were no shadows. Under the brush of the wild land
which I was skirting by now there seemed to be quite as
much of luminosity as overhead. The mist was the thinnest haze, and it seemed to derive its whiteness as much
from the virgin snow on the ground as from above. I
could not cease to marvel at this light which seemed to

be without a source—like the halo around the Saviour's face. The eye as yet did not reach very far, and wherever I looked, I found but one word to describe it: impalpable—and that is saying what it was not rather than what it was. As I said, there was no sunshine, but the light was there, omnipresent, diffused, coming mildly, softly, but from all sides, and out of all things as well as into them.

Shakespeare has this word in Macbeth, and I had often pondered on it:

> *So foul and fair a day I have not seen.*

This was it, I thought. We have such days about four or five times a year—and none but the northern countries have them. There are clouds—or rather, there is a uniform layer of cloud, very high, and just the slightest suggestion of curdiness in it; and the light is very white. These days seem to waken in me every wander instinct that lay asleep. There is nothing definite, nothing that seems to be emphasized—something seems to beckon to me and to invite me to take to my wings and just glide along—without beating of wings—as if I could glide without sinking, glide and still keep my height. . . . If you see the sun at all—as I did not on this day of days—he stands away up, very distant and quite aloof. He looks more like the moon than like his own self, white and heatless and lightless, as if it were not he at all from whom all this transparency and visibility proceeded.

I have lived in southern countries, and I have travelled rather far for a single lifetime. Like an epic stretch my memories into dim and ever receding pasts. I have drunk full and deep from the cup of creation. The Southern Cross is no strange sight to my eyes. I have slept in the desert close to my horse, and I have walked on Lebanon. I have cruised in the seven seas and seen the white marvels of ancient cities reflected in the wave of incredible

blueness. But then I was young. When the years began
to pile up, I longed to stake off my horizons, to flatten
out my views. I wanted the simpler, the more elemental
things, things cosmic in their associations, nearer to the
beginning or end of creation. The parrot that flashed
through "nutmeg groves" did not hold out so much
allurement as the simple grey-and-slaty junco. The
things that are unobtrusive and differentiated by shadings only—grey in grey above all—like our northern
woods, like our sparrows, our wolves—they held a more
compelling attraction than orgies of colour and screams
of sound. So I came home to the north. On days like this,
however, I should like once more to fly out and see the
tireless wave and the unconquerable rock. But I should
like to see them from afar and dimly only—as Moses
saw the promised land. Or I should like to point them
out to a younger soul and remark upon the futility and
innate vanity of things.

And because these days take me out of myself, because they change my whole being into a very indefinite
longing and dreaming, I wilfully blot from my vision
whatever enters. If I meet a tree, I see it not. If I meet a
man, I pass him by without speaking. I do not care to be
disturbed. I do not care to follow even a definite thought.
There is sadness in the mood, such sadness as enters—
strange to say—into a great and very definitely expected
disappointment. It is an exceedingly delicate sadness—
haughty, aloof like the sun, and like him cool to the outer
world. It does not even want sympathy; it merely wants
to be left alone.

It strangely chimed in with my mood on this particular and very perfect morning that no jolt shook me
up, that we glided along over virgin snow which had
come soft-footedly over night, in a motion so smooth and
silent as to suggest that wingless flight. . . .

We spurned the miles, and I saw them not. As if in

a dream we turned in at one of the "half-way farms," and
the horses drank. And we went on and wound our way
across that corner of the marsh. We came to the "White
Range Line House," and though there were many things
to see, I still closed the eye of conscious vision and saw
them not. We neared the bridge, and we crossed it; and
then—when I had turned southeast, on to the winding
log-road through the bush—at last the spell that was cast
over me gave way and broke. My horses fell into their
accustomed walk, and at last I saw.

Now, what I saw may not be worth the describing, I
do not know. It surely is hardly capable of being
described. But if I had been led through fairylands or
enchanted gardens, I could not have been awakened to
a truer day of joy, to a greater realization of the good
will towards all things than I was here.

Oh, the surpassing beauty of it! There stood the
trees, motionless under that veil of mist, and not their
slenderest finger but was clothed in white. And the white
it was! A translucent white, receding into itself, with
strange backgrounds of white behind it—a modest
white, and yet full of pride. An elusive white, and yet
firm and substantial. The white of a diamond lying on
snow-white velvet, the white of a diamond in diffused
light. None of the sparkle and colour play that the most
precious of stones assumes under a definite, limited light
which proceeds from a definite, limited source. Its
colour play was suggested, it is true, but so subdued that
you hardly thought of naming or even recognizing its
component parts. There was no red or yellow or blue or
violet, but merely that which might flash into red and
yellow and blue and violet, should perchance the sun
break forth and monopolize the luminosity of the atmosphere. There was, as it were, a latent opalescence.

And every twig and every bough, every branch and
every limb, every trunk and every crack even in the bark

was furred with it. It seemed as if the hoarfrost still continued to form. It looked heavy, and yet it was nearly without weight. Not a twig was bent down under its load, yet with its halo of frost it measured fully two inches across. The crystals were large, formed like spearheads, flat, slablike, yet of infinite thinness and delicacy, so thin and light that, when by misadventure my whip touched the boughs, the flakes seemed to float down rather than to fall. And every one of these flat and angular slabs was fringed with hairlike needles, or with featherlike needles, and longer needles stood in between. There was such an air of fragility about it all that you hated to touch it—and I, for one, took my whip down lest it shook bare too many boughs.

Whoever has seen the trees like that—and who has not?—will see with his mind's eye what I am trying to suggest rather than to describe. It was never the single sight nor the isolated thing that made my drives the things of beauty which they were. There was nothing remarkable in them either. They were commonplace enough. I really do not know why I should feel urged to describe our western winters. Whatever I may be able to tell you about them, is yours to see and yours to interpret. The gifts of Nature are free to all for the asking. And yet, so it seems to me, there is in the agglomerations of scenes and impressions, as they followed each other in my experience, something of the quality of a great symphony; and I consider this quality as a free and undeserved present which Chance or Nature shook out of her cornucopia so it happened to fall at my feet. I am trying to render this quality here for you.

On that short mile along the first of the east-west grades, before again I turned into the bush, I was for the thousandth time in my life struck with the fact how winter blots out the sins of utility. What is useful, is often ugly because in our fight for existence we do not always have time or effort to spare to consider the looks of things. But the slightest cover of snow will bury the eyesores. Snow is the greatest equalizer in Nature. No longer are there fields and wild lands, beautiful trails and ugly grades— all are hidden away under that which comes from Nature's purest hands and fertile thoughts alone. Now there was no longer the raw, offending scar on Nature's body; just a smooth expanse of snow-white ribbon that led afar.

That led afar! And here is a curious fact. On this early December morning—it was only a little after nine when I started the horses into their trot again—I noticed for the first time that this grade which sprang here out of the bush opened up to the east a vista into a seemingly endless distance. Twenty-six times I had gone along this piece of it, but thirteen times it had been at night, and thirteen times I had been facing west, when I went back to the scene of my work. So I had never looked east very far. This morning, however, in this strange light, which was at this very hour undergoing a subtle change that I could not define as yet, mile after mile of road seemed to lift itself up in the far-away distance, as if you might drive on for ever through fairyland. The very fact of its straightness, flanked as it was by the rows of frosted trees, seemed like a call. And a feeling that is very familiar to me—that of an eternity in the perpetuation of whatever may be the state I happen to be in, came over me, and a desire to go on and on, for ever, and to see what might be beyond. . . .

But then the turn into the bushy trail was reached. I did not see the slightest sign of it on the road. But Dan seemed infallible—he made the turn. And again I was in Winter's enchanted palace, again the slight whirl in the air that our motion set up made the fairy tracery of the boughs shower down upon me like snow-white petals of flowers, so delicate that to disturb the virginity of it all seemed like profaning the temple of the All-Highest.

But then I noticed that I had not been the first one to visit the woods. All over their soft-napped carpet floor there were the restless, fleeting tracks of the snowflake, lacing and interlacing in lines and loops, as if they had been assembled in countless numbers, as no doubt they had. And every track looked like nothing so much as like that kind of embroidery, done white upon white, which ladies, I think, call the feather stitch. In places I could clearly see how they had chased and pursued each other, running, and there was a merriness about their spoors, a suggestion of swiftness which made me look up and about to see whether they were not wheeling their restless curves and circles overhead. But in this I was disappointed for the moment, though only a little later I was to see them in numbers galore. It was on that last stretch of my road, when I drove along the dam of the angling ditch. There they came like a whirlwind and wheeled and curved and circled about as if they knew no enemy, feeding meanwhile with infallible skill from the tops of seed-bearing weeds while skimming along. But I am anticipating just now. In the bush I saw only their trails. Yet they suggested their twittering and whistling even there; and since on the gloomiest day their sound and their sight will cheer you, you surely cannot help feeling glad and overflowing with joy when you see any sign of them on a day like this!

Meanwhile we were winging along ourselves, so it seemed. For there was the second east-west grade ahead. And that made me think of wife and child to whom I was coming like Santa Claus, and so I stopped under a bush that overhung the trail; and though I hated to destroy even a trifling part of the beauty around, I reached high up with my whip and let go at the branches, so that the moment before the horses bolted, the flakes showered down upon me and my robes and the cutter and changed me into a veritable snowman in snow-white garb.

And then up on the grade. One mile to the east, and the bridge appeared.

It did not look like the work of man. Apart from its straight lines it resembled more the architecture of a forest brook as it will build after heavy fall rains followed by a late drought when all the waters of the wild are receding so that the icy cover stands above them like the arches of a bridge. It is strange how rarely the work of man will really harmonize with Nature. The beaver builds, and his work will blend. Man builds, and it jars— very likely because he mostly builds with silly pretensions. But in winter Nature breathes upon his handiwork and transforms it. Bridges may be imposing and of great artificial beauty in cities—as for instance the ancient structure that spans the Tiber just below the tomb of Hadrian, or among modern works the spider-web engineering feat of Brooklyn bridge—but if in the wilderness we run across them, there is something incongruous about them, and they disturb. Strange to say, there is the exception of highflung trellis-viaducts bridging the chasm of mountain canyons. Maybe it is exactly on account of their unpretentious, plain utility; or is it that they reconcile by their overweening boldness, by their very paradoxicality—as there is beauty even in the hawk's bloodthirsty savagery. To-day this bridge was, like the grades, like the trees and the meadows, furred over with opalescent, feathery frost.

And the dam over which I am driving now! This dam that erstwhile was a very blasphemy, an obscenity flung on the marshy meadows with their reeds, their cat-tails, and their wide-leaved swamp-dock clusters! It had been used by the winds as a veritable dumping ground for obnoxious weeds which grew and thrived on the marly clay while every other plant despised it! Not that I mean to decry weeds—far be it from me. When the goldenrod flings its velvet cushions along the edge of the copses, or when the dandelion spangles the meadows, they are things of beauty as well as any tulip or tiger-lily. But when they or their rivals, silverweed, burdock, false ragweed, thistles, gumweed, and others usurp the landscape and seem to choke up the very earth and the very air with ceaseless monotony and repetition, then they become an offence to the eye and a reproach to those who tolerate them. To-day, however, they all lent their stalks to support the hoarfrost, to double and quadruple its total mass. They were powdered over with countless diamonds.

It was here that I met with the flocks of snowflakes; and if my joyous mood had admitted of any enhancement, they would have given it.

And never before had I seen the school and the cottage from quite so far! The haze was still there, but somehow it seemed to be further overhead now, with a stratum of winter-clear air underneath. Once before, when driving along the first east-west grade, where I discovered the vista, I had wondered at the distance to which the eye could pierce. Here, on the dam, of course, my vision was further aided by the fact that whatever of trees and shrubs there was in the way—and a ridge of poplars ran at right angles to the ditch, throwing up a leafy curtain in summer—stood bare of its foliage. I was still nearly four miles from my "home" when I first beheld it. And how pitiably lonesome it looked! Not another house was to be seen in its neighbourhood. I touched the horses up with my whip. I felt as if I should fly across the distance and bring my presence to those in the cottage as their dearest gift. They knew I was coming. They were at this very moment flying to meet me with their thoughts. Was I well? Was I finding everything as I had wished to find it? And though I often told them how I loved and enjoyed my drives, they could not view them but with much anxiety, for they were waiting, waiting, waiting. . . . Waiting on Thursday for Friday to come, waiting on Wednesday and Tuesday and Monday—waiting on Sunday even, as soon as I had left; counting the days, and the hours, and the minutes, till I was out, fighting storm and night to my heart's content! And then—worry, worry, worry—what might not happen! Whatever my drives were to me, to them they were horrors. There never were watchers of weather and sky so anxiously eager as they! And when, as it often, too often happened, the winter storms came, when care rose, hope fell, then eye was clouded, thought dulled, heart aflutter. . . . Sometimes the soul sought comfort from nearest neighbours, and not always was it vouchsafed. "Well," they would say, "if he starts out to-day, he will kill his horses!"—or, "In weather like this I should not care to drive five miles!"—Surely, surely, I owe it to them, staunch, faithful hearts that they were, to set down this record so it may gladden the lonesome twilight hours that are sure to come. . . .

And at last I swung west again, up the ridge and on to the yard. And there on the porch stood the tall, young, smiling woman, and at her knee the fairest-haired girl in all the world. And quite unconscious of Nature's wonder-garb, though doubtlessly gladdened by it, the little girl shrilled out, "Oh, Daddy, Daddy, did du see Santa Claus?" And I replied lustily, "Of course, my girl, I am coming straight from his palace."

Chapter 4

SNOW

THE blizzard started on Wednesday morning. It was that rather common, truly western combination of a heavy snowstorm with a blinding northern gale—such as piles the snow in hills and mountains and makes walking next to impossible.

I cannot exactly say that I viewed it with unmingled joy. There were special reasons for that. It was the second week in January; when I had left "home" the Sunday before, I had been feeling rather bad; so my wife would worry a good deal, especially if I did not come at all. I knew there was such a thing as its becoming quite impossible to make the drive. I had been lost in a blizzard once or twice before in my lifetime. And yet, as long as there was the least chance that horse-power and human will-power combined might pull me through at all, I was determined to make or anyway to try it.

At noon I heard the first dismal warning. For some reason or other I had to go down into the basement of the school. The janitor, a highly efficient but exceedingly bad-humoured cockney, who was dissatisfied with all things Canadian because "in the old country we do things differently"—whose sharp tongue was feared by many, and who once remarked to a lady teacher in the most casual way, "If you was a lidy, I'd wipe my boots on you!"—this selfsame janitor, standing by the furnace, turned slowly around, showed his pale and hollow-eyed face, and smiled a withering and commiserating smile. "Ye won't go north this week," he remarked—not without sympathy, for somehow he had taken a liking to me, which even prompted him off and on to favour me with caustic expressions of what he thought of the school board and the leading citizens of the town. I, of course, never encouraged him in his communicativeness which seemed to be just what he would expect, and no rebuff ever goaded him into the slightest show of resentment. "We'll see," I said briefly. "Well, Sir," he repeated apodeictically, "ye won't." I smiled and went out.

But in my classroom I looked from the window across the street. Not even in broad daylight could you see the opposite houses or trees. And I knew that, once a storm like that sets in, it is apt to continue for days at a stretch. It was one of those orgies in which Titan Wind indulges every so often on our western prairies. I certainly needed something to encourage me, and so, before leaving the building, I went upstairs to the third story and looked through a window which faced north. But, though I was now above the drifting layer, I could not see very far here either; the snowflakes were small and like little round granules, hitting the panes of the windows with little sounds of "ping-ping"; and they came, driven by a relentless gale, in such numbers that they blotted out whatever was more than two or three hundred yards away.

The inhabitant of the middle latitudes of this continent has no data to picture to himself what a snow-storm in the north may be. To him snow is something benign that comes soft-footedly over night, and on the most silent wings like an owl, something that suggests the sleep of Nature rather than its battles. The further south you go, the more, of course, snow loses of its aggressive character.

At the dinner-table in the hotel I heard a few more disheartening words. But after four I defiantly got my tarpaulin out and carried it to the stable. If I had to run the risk of getting lost, at least I was going to prepare for it. I had once stayed out, snow-bound, for a day and a half, nearly without food and altogether without shelter; and I was not going to get thus caught again. I also carefully overhauled my cutter. Not a bolt but I tested it with a wrench; and before the stores were closed, I bought myself enough canned goods to feed me for a week should through any untoward accident the need arise. I always carried a little alcohol stove, and with my tarpaulin I could convert my cutter within three minutes into a windproof tent. Cramped quarters, to be sure, but better than being given over to the wind at thirty below!

More than any remark on the part of friends or acquaintances one fact depressed me when I went home. There was not a team in town which had come in from the country. The streets were deserted: the stores were empty. The north wind and the snow had the town to themselves.

On Thursday the weather was unchanged. On the way to the school I had to scale a snowdrift thrown up to a height of nearly six feet, and, though it was beginning to harden, from its own weight and the pressure of the wind, I still broke in at every step and found the task tiring in the extreme. I did my work, of course, as if nothing oppressed me, but in my heart I was beginning to face the possibility that, even if I tried, I might fail to reach my goal. The day passed by. At noon the schoolchildren, the teachers, and a few people hurrying to the post-office for their mail lent a fleeting appearance of life to the streets. It nearly cheered me; but soon after four the whole town again took on that deserted look which reminded me of an abandoned mining camp. The lights in the store windows had something artificial about them, as if they were merely painted on the canvas wings of a stage setting. Not a team came in all day.

On Friday morning the same. Burroughs would have said that the weather had gone into a rut. Still the wind whistled and howled through the bleak, dark, hollow dawn; the snow kept coming down and piling up, as if it could not be any otherwise. And as if to give notice of its intentions, the drift had completely closed up my front door. I fought my way to the school and thought things over. My wife and I had agreed, if ever the weather should be so bad that there was danger in going at night, I was to wait till Saturday morning and go by daylight. Neither one of us ever mentioned the possibility of giving the attempt up altogether. My wife probably understood that I would not bind myself by any such promise. Now even on this Friday I should have liked to go by night, if for no other reason, then for the experience's sake; but I reflected that I might get lost and not reach home at all. The horses knew the road—so long as there was any road; but there was none now. I felt it would not be fair to wife and child. So, reluctantly and with much hesitation, but definitely at last, I made up my mind that I was going to wait till morning. My cutter was ready—I had seen to that on Wednesday. As soon as the storm had set in, I had instinctively started to work in order to frustrate its designs.

At noon I met in front of the post-office a charming lady who with her husband and a young Anglican curate constituted about the only circle of real friends I had in town. "Why!" I exclaimed, "what takes you out into this storm, Mrs. ——?" "The desire," she gasped against the wind and yet in her inimitable way, as if she were asking a favour, "to have you come to our house for tea, my friend. You surely are not going this week?" "I am going to go to-morrow morning at seven," I said. "But I shall be delighted to have tea with you and Mr. ——." I read her at a glance. She knew that in not going out at night I should suffer—she wished to help me over the evening, so I should not feel too much thwarted, too helpless, and too lonesome. She smiled. "You really want to go? But I must not keep you. At six, if you please." And we went our ways without a salute, for none was possible at this gale-swept corner.

After four o'clock I took word to the stable to have my horses fed and harnessed by seven in the morning. The hostler had a tale to tell. "You going out north?" he enquired although he knew perfectly well I was. "Of course," I replied. "Well," he went on, "a man came in from ten miles out; he was half dead; come, look at his horses! He says, in places the snow is over the telephone posts." "I'll try it anyway," I said. "Just have the team ready. I know what I can ask my horses to do. If it cannot be done, I shall turn back, that is all."

When I stepped outside again, the wind seemed bent upon shaking the strongest faith. I went home to my house across the bridge and dressed. As soon as I was ready, I allowed myself to be swept past stable, past hotel and post-office till I reached the side street which led to the house where I was to be the guest.

How sheltered, homelike and protected everything looked inside. The hostess, as usual, was radiantly amiable. The host settled back after supper to talk old country. The Channel Islands, the French Coast, Kent and London—those were from common knowledge our most frequently recurring topics. Both host and hostess, that was easy to see, were bent upon beguiling the hours of their rather dark-humoured guest. But the howling gale outside was stronger than their good intentions. It was not very long before the conversation got around—reverted, so it seemed—to stories of storms, of being lost, of nearly freezing. The boys were sitting with wide and eager eyes, afraid they might be sent to bed before the feast of yarns was over. I told one or two of my most thrilling escapes, the host contributed a few more, and even the hostess had had an experience, driving on top of a railroad track for several miles, I believe, with a train, snowbound, behind her. I leaned over. "Mrs.

——," I said, "do not try to dissuade me. I am sorry to say it, but it is useless. I am bound to go." "Well," she said, "I wish you would not." "Thanks," I replied and looked at my watch. It was ten o'clock. "There is only one thing wrong with coming to have tea in this home," I continued and smiled; "it is so hard to say good-bye."

I carefully lighted my lantern and got into my wraps. The wind was howling dismally outside. For a moment we stood in the hall, shaking hands and paying the usual compliments; then one of the boys opened the door for me; and in stepping out I had one of the greatest surprises. Not far from the western edge of the world there stood the setting half-moon in a cloudless sky; myriads of stars were dusted over the vast, dark blue expanse, twinkling and blazing at their liveliest. And though the wind still whistled and shrieked and rattled, no snow came down, and not much seemed to drift. I pointed to the sky, smiled, nodded and closed the door. As far as the drifting of the snow went, I was mistaken, as I found out when I turned to the north, into the less sheltered street, past the post-office, hotel and stable. In front of a store I stopped to read a thermometer which I had found halfways reliable the year before. It read minus thirty-two degrees. . . .

It was still dark, of course, when I left the house on Saturday morning to be on my way. Also, it was cold, bitterly cold, but there was very little wind. In crossing the bridge which was swept nearly clean of snow I noticed a small, but somehow ominous-looking drift at the southern end. It had such a disturbed, lashed-up appearance. The snow was still loose, yet packed just hard enough to have a certain degree of toughness. You could no longer swing your foot through it: had you run into it at any great speed, you would have fallen; but as yet it was not hard enough to carry you. I knew that kind of a drift; it is treacherous. On a later drive one just

like it, only built on a vastly larger scale, was to lead to
the first of a series of little accidents which finally shat-
tered my nerve. That was the only time that my temerity
failed me. I shall tell you about that drive later on.

At the stable I went about my preparations in a
leisurely way. I knew that a supreme test was ahead of
myself and the horses, and I meant to have daylight for
tackling it. Once more I went over the most important
bolts; once more I felt and pulled at every strap in the
harness. I had a Clark footwarmer and made sure that it
functioned properly. I pulled the flaps of my military fur
cap down over neck, ears and cheeks. I tucked a pillow
under the sweater over my chest and made sure that my
leggings clasped my fur-lined moccasins well. Then, to
prevent my coat from opening even under the stress of
motion, just before I got into the cutter, I tied a rope
around my waist.

The hostler brought the horses into the shed. They
pawed the floor and snorted with impatience. While I
rolled my robes about my legs and drew the canvas curtain over the front part of the box, I weighed Dan with
my eyes. I had no fear for Peter, but Dan would have to
show to-day that he deserved the way I had fed and
nursed him. Like a chain, the strength of which is
measured by the strength of its weakest link, my team
was measured by Dan's pulling power and endurance.
But he looked good to me as he danced across the pole
and threw his head, biting back at Peter who was teasing
him.

The hostler was morose and in a biting mood. Every
motion of his seemed to say, "What is the use of all this?
No teamster would go out on a long drive in this
weather, till the snow has settled down; and here a
schoolmaster wants to try it."

At last he pushed the slide-doors aside, and we swung
out. I held the horses tight and drove them into that little

drift at the bridge to slow them down right from the start.

The dawn was white, but with a strictly localized angry glow where the sun was still hidden below the horizon. In a very few minutes he would be up, and I counted on making that first mile just before he appeared.

This mile is a wide, well-levelled road, but every so often, at intervals of maybe fifty to sixty yards, steep and long promontories of snow had been flung across—some of them five to six feet high. They started at the edge of the field to the left where a rank growth of shrubby weeds gave shelter for the snow to pile in. Their base, alongside the fence, was broad, and they tapered across the road, with a perfectly flat top, and with concave sides of a most delicate, smooth, and finished-looking curve, till at last they ran out into a sharp point, mostly beyond the road on the field to the right.

The wind plays strange pranks with snow; snow is the most plastic medium it has to mould into images and symbols of its moods. Here one of these promontories would slope down, and the very next one would slope upward as it advanced across the open space. In every case there had been two walls, as it were, of furious blow, and between the two a lane of comparative calm, caused by the shelter of a clump of brush or weeds, in which the snow had taken refuge from the wind's rough and savage play. Between these capes of snow there was an occasional bare patch of clean swept ground. Altogether there was an impression of barren, wild, bitter-cold windiness about the aspect that did not fail to awe my mind; it looked inhospitable, merciless, and cruelly playful.

As yet the horses seemed to take only delight in dashing through the drifts, so that the powdery crystals flew aloft and dusted me all over. I peered across the field to the left, and a curious sight struck me. There was apparently no steady wind at all, but here and there, and every now and then, a little whirl of snow would rise and fall again. Every one of them looked for all the world like a rabbit reconnoitring in deep grass. It jumps up on its hindlegs, while running, peers out, and settles down again. It was as if the snow meant to have a look at me, the interloper at such an early morning hour. The snow was so utterly dry that it obeyed the lightest breath; and whatever there was of motion in the air, could not amount to more than a cat's-paw's sudden reach.

At the exact moment when the snow where it stood up highest became suffused with a rose-red tint from the rising sun, I arrived at the turn to the correction line. Had I been a novice at the work I was engaged in, the sight that met my eye might well have daunted me. Such drifts as I saw here should be broken by drivers who have short hauls to make before the long-distance traveller attempts them. From the fence on the north side of the road a smoothly curved expanse covered the whole of the road allowance and gently sloped down into the field at my left. Its north edge stood like a cliff, the exact height of the fence, four feet I should say. In the centre it rose to probably six feet and then fell very gradually, whaleback fashion, to the south. Not one of the fence posts to the left was visible. The slow emergence of the tops of these fence posts became during the following week, when I drove out here daily, a measure for me of the settling down of the drift. I believe I can say from my observations that if no new snow falls or drifts in, and if no very considerable evaporation takes place, a newly piled snowdrift, undisturbed except by wind-pressure, will finally settle down to about from one-third to one-half of its original height, according to the pressure of the wind that was behind the snow when it first was thrown down. After it has, in this contracting process, reached two-thirds of its first height, it can usually be relied upon to carry horse and man.

The surface of this drift, which covered a ditch besides the grade and its grassy flanks, showed that curious appearance that we also find in the glaciated surfaces of granite rock and which, in them, geologists call exfoliation. In the case of rock it is the consequence of extreme changes in temperature. The surface sheet in expanding under sudden heat detaches itself in large leaflike layers. In front of my wife's cottage up north there lay an exfoliated rock in which I watched the process for a number of years. In snow, of course, the origin of this appearance is entirely different; snow is laid down in layers by the waves in the wind. "Adfoliation" would be a more nearly correct appellation of the process. But from the analogy of the appearance I shall retain the more common word and call it exfoliation. Layers upon layers of paperlike sheets are superimposed upon each other, their edges often "cropping out" on sloping surfaces; and since these edges, according to the curvatures of the surfaces, run in wavy lines, the total aspect is very often that of "moire" silk.

I knew the road as well as I had ever known a road. In summer there was a grassy expanse some thirty feet wide to the north; then followed the grade, flanked to the south by a ditch; and the tangle of weeds and small brush beyond reached right up to the other fence. I had to stay on or rather above the grade; so I stood up and selected the exact spot where to tackle it. Later, I knew, this drift would be harmless enough; there was sufficient local traffic here to establish a well-packed trail. At present, however, it still seemed a formidable task for a team that was to pull me over thirty-three miles more. Besides it was a first test for my horses; I did not know yet how they would behave in snow.

But we went at it. For a moment things happened too

fast for me to watch details. The horses plunged wildly
and reared on their hind feet in a panic, straining against
each other, pulling apart, going down underneath the
pole, trying to turn and retrace their steps. And meanwhile the cutter went sharply up at first, as if on the crest
of a wave, then toppled over into a hole made by Dan,
and altogether behaved like a boat tossed on a stormy
sea. Then order returned into the chaos. I had the lines
short, wrapped double and treble around my wrists; my
feet stood braced in the corner of the box, knees touching the dashboard; my robes slipped down. I spoke to the
horses in a soft, quiet, purring voice; and at last I pulled
in. Peter hated to stand. I held him. Then I looked back.
This first wild plunge had taken us a matter of two hundred yards into the drift. Peter pulled and champed at
the bit; the horses were sinking nearly out of sight. But
I knew that many and many a time in the future I should
have to go through just this, and that from the beginning
I must train the horses to tackle it right. So, in spite of
my aching wrists I kept them standing till I thought that
they were fully breathed. Then I relaxed my pull the
slightest bit and clicked my tongue. "Good," I thought,
"they are pulling together!" And I managed to hold
them in line. They reared and plunged again like drowning things in their last agony, but they no longer clashed
against nor pulled away from each other. I measured
the distance with my eye. Another two hundred yards or
thereabout, and I pulled them in again. Thus we stopped
altogether four times. The horses were steaming when
we got through this drift which was exactly half a mile
long; my cutter was packed level full with slabs and
clods of snow; and I was pretty well exhausted myself.

"If there is very much of this," I thought for the
moment, "I may not be able to make it." But then I
knew that a north-south road will drift in badly only
under exceptional circumstances. It is the east-west

grades that are most apt to give trouble. Not that I minded my part of it, but I did not mean to kill my horses. I had sized them up in their behaviour towards snow. Peter, as I had expected, was excitable. It was hard to recognize in him just now, as he walked quietly along, the uproar of playing muscle and rearing limbs that he had been when we first struck the snow. That was well and good for a short, supreme effort; but not even for Peter would it do in the long, endless drifts which I had to expect. Dan was quieter, but he did not have Peter's staying power; in fact, he was not really a horse for the road. Strange, in spite of his usual keenness on the level road, he seemed to show more snow sense in the drift. This was to be amply confirmed in the future. Whenever an accident happened, it was Peter's fault. As you will see if you read on, Dan once lay quiet when Peter stood right on top of him.

On this road north I found the same "promontories" that had been such a feature of the first one, flung across from the northwest to the southeast. Since the clumps of shrubs to the left were larger here, and more numerous, too, the drifts occasionally also were larger and higher; but not one of them was such that the horses could not clear it with one or two leaps. The sun was climbing, the air was winter-clear and still. None of the farms which I passed showed the slightest sign of life. I had wrapped up again and sat in comparative comfort and at ease, enjoying the clear sparkle and glitter of the virgin snow. It was not till considerably later that the real significance of the landscape dawned upon my consciousness. Still there was even now in my thoughts a speculative undertone. Subconsciously I wondered what might be ahead of me.

We made Bell's corner in good time. The mile to the west proved easy. There were drifts, it is true, and the going was heavy, but at no place did the snow for any length of time reach higher than the horses' hocks. We turned to the north again, and here, for a while, the road was very good indeed; the underbrush to the left, on those expanses of wild land, had fettered, as it were, the feet of the wind. The snow was held everywhere, and very little of it had drifted. Only one spot I remember where a clump of Russian willow close to the trail had offered shelter enough to allow the wind to fill in the narrow road-gap to a depth of maybe eight or nine feet; but here it was easy to go around to the west. Without any further incident we reached the point where the useless, supernumerary fencepost had caught my eye on my first trip out. I had made nearly eight miles now.

But right here I was to get my first inkling of sights that might shatter my nerve. You may remember that a grove of tall poplars ran to the east, skirted along its southern edge by a road and a long line of telephone posts. Now here, in this shelter of the poplars, the snow from the more or less level and unsheltered spaces to the northwest had piled in indeed. It sloped up to the east; and never shall I forget what I beheld.

The first of the posts stood a foot in snow; at the second one the drift reached six or seven feet up; the next one looked only half as long as the first one, and you might have imagined, standing as it did on a sloping hillside, that it had intentionally been made so much shorter than the others; but at the bottom of the visible part the wind, in sweeping around the pole, had scooped out a funnel-shaped crater which seemed to open into the very earth like a sinkhole. The next pole stood like a giant buried up to his chest and looked singularly helpless and footbound; and the last one I saw showed just its crossbar with three glassy, green insulators above the mountain of snow. The whole surface of this gigantic drift showed again that "exfoliated" appearance which I have described. Strange to say, this very exfoliation gave it something of a quite peculiarly desolate aspect. It looked so harsh, so millennial-old, so antediluvian and pre-Adamic! I still remember with particular distinctness the slight dizziness that overcame me, the sinking feeling in my heart, the awe, and the foreboding that I had challenged a force in Nature which might defy all tireless effort and the most fearless heart.

So the hostler had not been fibbing after all!

But not for a moment did I think of turning back. I am fatalistic in temperament. What is to be, is to be, that is not my outlook. If at last we should get bound up in a drift, well and good, I should then see what the next move would have to be. While the wind blows, snow drifts; while my horses could walk and I was not disabled, my road led north, not south. Like the snow I obeyed the laws of my nature. So far the road was good, and we swung along.

Somewhere around here a field presented a curious view. Its crop had not been harvested; it still stood in stooks. But from my side I saw nothing of the sheaves— it seemed to be flax, for here and there a flag of loose heads showed at the top. The snow had been blown up from all directions, so it looked, by the counter-currents that set up in the lee of every obstacle. These mounds presented one and all the appearance of cones or pyramids of butter patted into shape by upward strokes made with a spoon. There were the sharp ridges, irregular and erratic, and there were the hollows running up their flanks—exactly as such a cone of butter will show them. And the whole field was dotted with them, as if there were so many fresh graves.

I made the twelve-mile bridge—passing through the cottonwood gate—reached the "hovel," and dropped into the wilderness again. Here the bigger trees stood strangely bare. Winter reveals the bark and the "habit" of trees. All ornaments and unessentials have been dropped. The naked skeletons show. I remember how I was more than ever struck by that dappled appearance of the bark of the balm: an olive-green, yellowish hue, ridged and spotted with the black of ancient, overgrown leaf-scars; there was actually something gay about it; these poplars are certainly beautiful winter trees. The aspens were different. Although their stems stood white on white in the snow, that greenish tinge in their white gave them a curious look. From the picture that I carry about in my memory of this morning I cannot help the impression that they looked as if their white were not natural at all; they looked whitewashed! I have often since confirmed this impression when there was snow on the ground.

In the copses of saplings the zigzagging of the boles from twig to twig showed very distinctly, more so, I believe, than to me it had ever done before. How slender and straight they look in their summer garb—now they were stripped, and bone and sinew appeared.

We came to the "half-way farms," and the marsh lay ahead. I watered the horses, and I do not know what made me rest them for a little while, but I did. On the yard of the farm where I had turned in there was not a soul to be seen. Barns and stables were closed—and I noticed that the back door of the dwelling was buried tight by the snow. No doubt everybody preferred the neighbourhood of the fire to the cold outside. While stopping, I faced for the first time the sun. He was high in the sky by now—it was half past ten—and it suddenly came home to me that there was something relentless, inexorable, cruel, yes, something of a sneer in the pitiless way in which he looked down on the infertile waste around. Unaccountably two Greek words formed on my lips: Homer's *pontos atrygetos*—the barren sea. Half an hour later I was to realize the significance of it.

I turned back to the road and north again. For

another half mile the fields continued on either side; but
somehow they seemed to take on a sinister look. There
was more snow on them than I had found on the level
land further south; the snow lay more smoothly, again
under those "exfoliated" surface sheets which here, too,
gave it an inhuman, primeval look; in the higher sun the
vast expanse looked, I suppose, more blindingly white;
and nowhere did buildings or thickets seem to emerge.
Yet, so long as the grade continued, the going was fair
enough.

Then I came to the corner which marked half the distance, and there I stopped. Right in front, where the
trail had been and where a ditch had divided off the
marsh, a fortress of snow lay now: a seemingly im-
pregnable bulwark, six or seven feet high, with rounded
top, fitting descriptions which I had read of the underground bomb-proofs around Belgian strongholds—those
forts which were hammered to pieces by the Germans in
their first, heart-breaking forward surge in 1914. There
was not a wrinkle in this inverted bowl. There it lay,
smooth and slick—curled up in security, as it were, some
twenty, thirty feet across; and behind it others, and more
of them to the right and to the left. This had been a
stretch covered with brush and bush, willow and poplar
thickets; but my eye saw nothing except a mammiferous
waste, cruelly white, glittering in the heatless, chuckling
sun, and scoffing at me, the intruder. I stood up again
and peered out. To the east it seemed as if these buttes
of snow were a trifle lower; but maybe the ground underneath also sloped down. I wished I had travelled here
more often by daytime, so I might know. As it was, there
was nothing for it; I had to tackle the task. And we
plunged in.

I had learned something from my first experience in
the drift one mile north of town, and I kept my horses
well under control. Still, it was a wild enough dash.

Peter lost his footing two or three times and worked himself into a mild panic. But Dan—I could not help admiring the way in which, buried over his back in snow, he would slowly and deliberately rear on his hindfeet and take his bound. For fully five minutes I never saw anything of the horses except their heads. I inferred their motions from the dusting snowcloud that rose above their bodies and settled on myself. And then somehow we emerged. We reached a stretch of ground where the snow was just high enough to cover the hocks of the horses. It was a hollow scooped out by some freak of the wind. I pulled in, and the horses stood panting. Peter no longer showed any desire to fret and to jump. Both horses apparently felt the wisdom of sparing their strength. They were all white with the frost of their sweat and the spray of the snow.

While I gave them their time, I looked around, and here a lesson came home to me. In the hollow where we stood, the snow did not lie smoothly. A huge obstacle to the northwest, probably a buried clump of brush, had made the wind turn back upon itself, first downward, then, at the bottom of the pit, in a direction opposite to that of the main current above, and finally slantways upward again to the summit of the obstacle, where it rejoined the parent blow. The floor of the hollow was cleanly scooped out and chiselled in low ridges; and these ridges came from the southeast, running their points to the northwest. I learned to look out for this sign, and I verily believe that, had I not learned that lesson right now, I should never have reached the creek which was still four or five miles distant.

The huge mound in the lee of which I was stopping was a matter of two hundred yards away; nearer to it the snow was considerably deeper; and since it presented an appearance very characteristic of prairie bush-drifts, I shall describe it in some detail. Apparently the winds

had first bent over all the stems of the clump; for whenever I saw one of them from the north, it showed a
smooth, clean upward sweep. On the south side the snow
first fell in a sheer cliff; then there was a hollow which
was partly filled by a talus-shaped drift thrown in by the
counter currents from the southern pit in which we were
stopping; the sides of this talus again showed the marks
that reminded of those left by the spoon when butter is
roughly stroked into the shape of a pyramid. The interesting parts of the structure consisted in the beetling
brow of the cliff and the roof of the cavity underneath.
The brow had a honeycombed appearance; the snow had
been laid down in layers of varying density (I shall dis-
cuss this more fully in the next chapter when we are
going to look in on the snow while it is actually at work);
and the counter currents that here swept upward in a
slanting direction had bitten out the softer layers, leaving a fine network of little ridges which reminded
strangely of the delicate fretwork-tracery in wind-sculp-
tured rock—as I had seen it in the Black Hills in South
Dakota. This piece of work of the wind is exceedingly
short-lived in snow, and it must not be confounded with
the honeycombed appearance of those faces of snow
cliffs which are "rotting" by reason of their exposure to
the heat of the noonday sun. These latter are coarse,
often dirty, and nearly always have something bristling
about them which is entirely absent in the sculptures of
the wind. The under side of the roof in the cavity looked
very much as a very stiff or viscid treacle would look
when spread over a meshy surface, as, for instance, over
a closely woven netting of wire. The stems and the
branches of the brush took the place of the wire, and in
their meshes the snow had been pressed through by its
own weight, but held together by its curious ductility or
tensile strength of which I was to find further evidence
soon enough. It thus formed innumerable, blunted little

stalactites, but without the corresponding stalagmites which you find in limestone caves or on the north side of buildings when the snow from the roof thaws and forms icicles and slender cones of ice growing up to meet them from the ground where the trickling drops fall and freeze again.

By the help of these various tokens I had picked my next resting place before we started up again. It was on this second dash that I understood why those Homeric words had come to my lips a while ago. This was indeed like nothing so much as like being out on rough waters and in a troubled sea, with nothing to brace the storm with but a wind-tossed nutshell of a one-man sailing craft. I knew that experience for having out-ridden many a gale in the mouth of the mighty St. Lawrence River. When the snow reached its extreme in depth, it gave you the feeling which a drowning man may have when fighting his desperate fight with the salty waves. But more impressive than that was the frequent outer resemblance. The waves of the ocean rise up and reach out and batter against the rocks and battlements of the shore, retreating again and ever returning to the assault, covering the obstacles thrown in the way of their progress with thin sheets of licking tongues at least. And if such a high crest wave had suddenly been frozen into solidity, its outline would have mimicked to perfection many a one of the snow shapes that I saw around.

Once the horses had really learned to pull exactly together—and they learned it thoroughly here—our progress was not too bad. Of course, it was not like going on a grade, be it ever so badly drifted in. Here the ground underneath, too, was uneven and overgrown with a veritable entanglement of brush in which often the horses' feet would get caught. As for the road, there was none left, nothing that even by the boldest stretch of imagination could have been considered even as the slightest indication of one. And worst of all, I knew positively that there would be no trail at any time during the winter. I was well aware of the fact that, after it once snowed up, nobody ever crossed this waste between the "half-way farms" and the "White Range Line House." This morning it took me two and a half solid hours to make four miles.

But the ordeal had its reward. Here where the fact that there was snow on the ground, and plenty of it, did no longer need to be sunk into my brain—as soon as it had lost its value as a piece of news and a lesson—I began to enjoy it just as the hunter in India will enjoy the battle of wits when he is pitted against a yellow-black tiger. I began to catch on to the ways of this snow; I began, as it were, to study the mentality of my enemy. Though I never kill, I am after all something of a sportsman. And still another thing gave me back that mental equilibrium which you need in order to see things and to reason calmly about them. Every dash of two hundred yards or so brought me that much nearer to my goal. Up to the "half-way farms" I had, as it were, been working uphill : there was more ahead than behind. This was now reversed : there was more behind than ahead, and as yet I did not worry about the return trip.

Now I have already said that snow is the only really plastic element in which the wind can carve the vagaries of its mood and leave a record of at least some permanency. The surface of the sea is a wonderful book to be read with a lightning-quick eye; I do not know anything better to do as a cure for ragged nerves—provided you are a good sailor. But the forms are too fleeting, they change too quickly—so quickly, indeed, that I have never succeeded in so fixing their record upon my memory as to be able to develop one form from the other in descriptive notes. It is that very fact, I believe, upon which hinges the curative value of the sight : you are so

completely absorbed by the moment, and all other things
fall away. Many and many a day have I lain in my deck
chair on board a liner and watched the play of the
waves; but the pleasure, which was very great indeed,
was momentary; and sometimes, when in an unsym-
pathetic mood, I have since impatiently wondered in
what that fascination may have consisted. It was different here. Snow is very nearly as yielding as water and,
once it fully responds in its surface to the carving forces
of the wind, it stays—as if frozen into the glittering
marble image of its motion. I know few things that are
as truly fascinating as the sculptures of the wind in snow;
for here you have time and opportunity a-plenty to probe
not only into the what, but also into the why. Maybe
that one day I shall write down a fuller account of my
observations. In this report I shall have to restrict myself to a few indications, for this is not the record of the
whims of the wind, but merely the narrative of my drives.

In places, for instance, the rounded, "bomb-proof"
aspect of the expanses would be changed into the distinct contour of gigantic waves with a very fine, very
sharp crest-line. The upsweep from the northwest would
be ever so slightly convex, and the downward sweep into
the trough was always very distinctly concave. This was
not the ripple which we find in beach sand. That ripple
was there, too, and in places it covered the wide backs of
these huge waves all over; but never was it found on the
concave side. Occasionally, but rarely, one of these great
waves would resemble a large breaker with a curly crest.
Here the onward sweep from the northwest had built the
snow out, beyond the supporting base, into a thick overhanging ledge which here and there had sagged; but by
virtue of that tensile strength and cohesion in snow
which I have mentioned already, it still held together
and now looked convoluted and ruffled in the most de-
ceiving way. I believe I actually listened for the muffled

roar which the breaker makes when its subaqueous part begins to sweep the upward-sloping beach. To make this illusion complete, or to break it by the very absurdity and exaggeration of a comparison drawn out too far—I do not know which—there would, every now and then, from the crest of one of these waves, jut out something which closely resembled the wide back of a large fish diving down into the concave side towards the trough. This looked very much like porpoises or dolphins jumping in a heaving sea; only that in my memory picture the real dolphins always jump in the opposite direction, against the run of the waves, bridging the trough.

In other places a fine, exceedingly delicate crest-line would spring up from the high point of some buried obstacle and sweep along in the most graceful curve as far as the eye would carry. I particularly remember one of them, and I could discover no earthly reason for the curvature in it.

Again there would be a triangular—or should I say "tetrahedral"?—up-sweep from the direction of the wind, ending in a sharp, perfectly plane down-sweep on the south side; and the point of this three-sided but oblique pyramid would hang over like the flap of a tam. There was something of the consistency of very thick cloth about this overhanging flap.

Or an up-slope from the north would end in a long, nearly perpendicular cliff-line facing south. And the talus formation which I have mentioned would be perfectly smooth; but it did not reach quite to the top of the cliff, maybe to within a foot of it. The upsloping layer from the north would hang out again, with an even brow; but between this smooth cornice and the upper edge of the talus the snow looked as if it had been squeezed out by tremendous pressure from above, like an exceedingly viscid liquid—cooling glue, for instance, which is being squeezed out from between the core and the veneer in a veneering press.

Once I passed close to, and south of, two thickets which were completely buried by the snow. Between them a ditch had been scooped out in a very curious fashion. It resembled exactly a winding river bed with its water drained off; it was two or three feet deep, and wherever it turned, its banks were undermined on the "throw" side by the "wash" of the furious blow. The analogy between the work of the wind and the work of flowing water constantly obtrudes, especially where this work is one of "erosion."

But as flowing water will swing up and down in the most surprising forms where the bed of the river is rough with rocks and throws it into choppy waves which do not seem to move, so the snow was thrown up into the most curious forms where the frozen swamp ground underneath had bubbled, as it were, into phantastic shapes. I remember several places where a perfect circle was formed by a sharp crestline that bounded a hemispherical, crater-like hollow. When steam bubbles up through thick porridge, in its leisurely and impeded way, and the bubble bursts with a clucking sound, then for a moment a crater is formed just like these circular holes; only here in the snow they were on a much larger scale, of course, some of them six to ten feet in diameter.

And again the snow was thrown up into a bulwark, twenty and more feet high, with that always repeating cliff-face to the south, resembling a miniature Gibraltar, with many smaller ones of most curiously similar form on its back: bulwarks upon bulwarks, all lowering to the south. In these the aggressive nature of storm-flung snow was most apparent. They were formidable structures; formidable and intimidating, more through the suggestiveness of their shape than through mere size.

I came to places where the wind had had its moments

of frolicsome humour, where it had made grim fun of its own massive and cumbersome and yet so pliable and elastic majesty. It had turned around and around, running with breathless speed, with its tongue lolling out, as it were, and probably yapping and snapping in mocking mimicry of a pup trying to catch its tail; and it had scooped out a spiral trough with overhanging rim. I felt sorry that I had not been there to watch it, because after all, what I saw was only the dead record of something that had been very much alive and vociferatingly noisy. And in another place it had reared and raised its head like a boa constrictor, ready to strike at its prey; up to the flashing, forked tongue it was there. But one spot I remember, where it looked exactly as if quite consciously it had attempted the outright ludicrous: it had thrown up the snow into the semblance of some formidable animal—more like a gorilla than anything else it looked, a gorilla that stands on its four hands and raises every hair on its back and snarls in order to frighten that which it is afraid of itself—a leopard maybe.

And then I reached the "White Range Line House." Curiously enough, there it stood, sheltered by its majestic bluff to the north, as peaceful looking as if there were no such a thing as that record, which I had crossed, of the uproar and fury of one of the forces of Nature engaged in an orgy. And it looked so empty, too, and so deserted, with never a wisp of smoke curling from its flue-pipe, that for a moment I was tempted to turn in and see whether maybe the lonely dweller was ill. But then I felt as if I could not be burdened with any stranger's worries that day.

The effective shelter of the poplar forest along the creek made itself felt. The last mile to the northeast was peaceful driving. I felt quite cheered, though I walked the horses over the whole of the mile since both began to show signs of wear. The last four miles had been a test to

try any living creature's mettle. To me it had been one
of the culminating points in that glorious winter, but the
horses had lacked the mental stimulus, and even I felt
rather exhausted.

On the bridge I stopped, threw the blankets over the
horses, and fed. Somehow this seemed to be the best
place to do it. There was no snow to speak of, and I did
not know yet what might follow. The horses were drooping, and I gave them an additional ten minutes' rest.
Then I slowly made ready. I did not really expect any
serious trouble.

We turned at a walk, and the chasm of the bush road
opened up. Instantly I pulled the horses in. What I saw,
baffled me for a moment so completely that I just sat
there and gasped. There was no road. The trees to both
sides were not so overly high, but the snow had piled in
level with their tops; the drift looked like a gigantic
barricade. It was that fleeting sight of the telephone posts
over again, though on a slightly smaller scale; but this
time it was in front. Slowly I started to whistle and then
looked around. I remembered now. There was a newly
cut-out road running north past the school which lay
embedded in the bush. It had offered a lane to the wind;
and the wind, going there, in cramped space, at a doubly
furious stride, had picked up and carried along all the
loose snow from the grassy glades in its path. The road
ended abruptly just north of the drift, where the east-
west grade sprang up. When the wind had reached this
end of the lane, where the bush ran at right angles to its
direction, it had found itself in something like a blind
alley, and, sweeping upward, to clear the obstacle, it had
dropped every bit of its load into the shelter of the brush,
gradually, in the course of three long days, building up
a ridge that buried underbrush and trees. I might have
known it, of course. I knew enough about snow; all the
conditions for an exceptionally large drift were provided

for here. But it had not occurred to me, especially after
I had found the northern fringe of the marsh so well
sheltered. Here I felt for a moment as if all the snow of
the universe had piled in. As I said, I was so completely
baffled that I could have turned the horses then and
there.

But after a minute or two my eyes began to cast about.
I turned to the south, right into the dense underbrush
and towards the creek which here swept south in a long,
flat curve. Peter was always intolerant of anything
that moved underfoot. He started to bolt when the dry
and hard-frozen stems snapped and broke with reports
resembling pistol shots. But since Dan kept quiet, I held
Peter well in hand. I went along the drift for maybe
three to four hundred yards, reconnoitring. Then the trees
began to stand too dense for me to proceed without en-
dangering my cutter. Just beyond I saw the big trough
of the creek bed, and though I could not make out how
conditions were at its bottom, the drift continued on its
southern bank, and in any case it was impossible to cross
the hollow. So I turned; I had made up my mind to try
the drift.

About a hundred and fifty yards from the point where
I had turned off the road there was something like a
fold in the flank of the drift. At its foot I stopped. For
a moment I tried to explain that fold to myself. This
is what I arrived at. North of the drift, just about where
the new cut-out joined the east-west grade, there was a
small clearing caused by a bush fire which a few years
ago had penetrated thus far into this otherwise virgin
corner of the forest. Unfortunately it stood so full of
charred stumps that it was impossible to get through
there. But the main currents of the wind would have free
play in this opening, and I knew that, when the blizzard
began, it had been blowing from a more northerly
quarter than later on, when it veered to the northwest.

And though the snow came careering along the lane of the cut-out, that is, from due north, its "throw" and therefore the direction of the drift would be determined by the direction of the wind that took charge of it on this clearing. Probably, then, a first, provisional drift whose long axis lay nearly in a north-south line, had been piled up by the first, northerly gale. Later a second, larger drift had been superimposed upon it at an angle, with its main axis running from the northwest to the southeast. The fold marked the point where the first, smaller drift still emerged from the second larger one. This reasoning was confirmed by a study of the clearing itself which I came to make two or three weeks after.

Before I called on the horses to give me their very last ounce of strength, I got out of my cutter once more and made sure that my lines were still sound. I trusted my ability to guide the horses even in this crucial test, but I dreaded nothing so much as that the lines might break; and I wanted to guard against any accident. I should mention that, of course, the top of my cutter was down, that the traces of the harness were new, and that the cutter itself during its previous trials had shown an exceptional stability. Once more I thus rested my horses for five minutes; and they seemed to realize what was coming. Their heads were up, their ears were cocked. When I got back into my cutter, I carefully brushed the snow from moccasins and trousers, laid the robe around my feet, adjusted my knees against the dashboard, and tied two big loops into the lines to hold them by.

Then I clicked my tongue. The horses bounded upward in unison. For a moment it looked as if they intended to work through, instead of over, the drift. A wild shower of angular snow-slabs swept in upon me. The cutter reared up and plunged and reared again—and then the view cleared. The snow proved harder than I had anticipated—which bespoke the fury of the blow that had piled it. It did not carry the horses, but neither —once we had reached a height of five or six feet—did they sink beyond their bellies and out of sight. I had no eye for anything except them. What lay to right or left, seemed not to concern me. I watched them work. They went in bounds, working beautifully together. Rhythmically they reared, and rhythmically they plunged. I had dropped back to the seat, holding them with a firm hand, feet braced against the dashboard; and whenever they got ready to rear, I called to them in a low and quiet voice, "Peter—Dan—now!" And their muscles played with the effort of desperation. It probably did not take more than five minutes, maybe considerably less, before we had reached the top, but to me it seemed like hours of nearly fruitless endeavour. I did not realize at first that we were high. I shall never forget the weird kind of astonishment when the fact came home to me that what snapped and crackled in the snow under the horses' hoofs, were the tops of trees. Nor shall the feeling of estrangement, as it were—as if I were not myself, but looking on from the outside at the adventure of somebody who yet was I—the feeling of other-worldliness, if you will pardon the word, ever fade from my memory—a feeling of having been carried beyond my depth where I could not swim—which came over me when with two quick glances to right and left I took in the fact that there were no longer any trees to either side, that I was above that forest world which had so often engulfed me.

Then I drew my lines in. The horses fought against it, did not want to stand. But I had to find my way, and while they were going, I could not take my eyes from them. It took a supreme effort on my part to make them obey. At last they stood, but I had to hold them with all my strength, and with not a second's respite. Now that I was on top of the drift, the problem of how to get down loomed larger than that of getting up had seemed before. I knew I did not have half a minute in which to decide upon my course; for it became increasingly difficult to hold the horses back, and they were fast sinking away.

During this short breathing spell I took in the situation. We had come up in a northeast direction, slanting along the slope. Once on top, I had instinctively turned to the north. Here the drift was about twenty feet wide, perfectly level and with an exfoliated surface layer. To the east the drift fell steeply, with a clean, smooth cliff-line marking off the beginning of the descent; this line seemed particularly disconcerting, for it betrayed the concave curvature of the down-sweep. A few yards to the north I saw below, at the foot of the cliff, the old logging-trail, and I noticed that the snow on it lay as it had fallen, smooth and sheer, without a ripple of a drift. It looked like mockery. And yet that was where I had to get down.

The next few minutes are rather a maze in my memory. But two pictures were photographed with great distinctness. The one is of the moment when we went over the edge. For a second Peter reared up, pawing the air with his forefeet; Dan tried to back away from the empty fall. I had at this excruciating point no purchase whatever on the lines. Then apparently Peter sat or fell down, I do not know which, on his haunches and began to slide. The cutter lurched to the left as if it were going to spill all it held. Dan was knocked off his hind feet by the drawbar—and we plunged. . . . We came to with a terrific jolt that sent me in a heap against the dashboard. One jump, and I stood on the ground. The cutter—and this is the second picture which is etched clearly on the plate of my memory—stood on its pole, leaning at an angle of forty-five degrees against the drift. The horses were as if stunned. "Dan, Peter!" I shouted, and they struggled to their feet. They were badly winded, but otherwise everything seemed all right. I looked wistfully back and up at the gully which we had torn into the flank of the drift.

I should gladly have breathed the horses again, but they were hot, the air was at zero or colder, the rays of the sun had begun to slant. I walked for a while alongside the team. They were drooping sadly. Then I got in again, driving them slowly till we came to the crossing of the ditch. I had no eye for the grade ahead. On the bush road the going was good—now and then a small drift, but nothing alarming anywhere. The anti-climax had set in. Again the speckled trunks of the balm poplars struck my eye, now interspersed with the scarlet stems of the red osier dogwood. But they failed to cheer me—they were mere facts, unable to stir moods. . . .

I began to think. A few weeks ago I had met that American settler with the French-sounding name who lived alongside the angling dam further north. We had talked snow, and he had said, "Oh, up here it never is bad except along this grade";—we were stopping on the last east-west grade, the one I was coming to—"there you cannot get through. You'd kill your horses. Level with the tree-tops." Well, I had had just that a little while ago—I could not afford any more of it. So I made up my mind to try a new trail, across a section which was fenced. It meant getting out of my robes twice more, to open the gates, but I preferred that to another tree-high drift. To spare my horses was now my only consideration. I should not have liked to take the new trail by night, for fear of missing the gates; but that objection did not hold just now. Horses and I were pretty well spent. So, instead of forking off the main trail to the north we went straight ahead.

In due time I came to the bridge which I had to cross in order to get up on the dam. Here I saw—in an

absent-minded, half unconscious, and uninterested way
—one more structure built by architect wind. The deep
master ditch from the north emptied here, to the left of
the bridge, into the grade ditch which ran east and west.
And at the corner the snow had very nearly bridged it—
so nearly that you could easily have stepped across the
remaining gap. But below it was hollow—nothing sup-
ported the bridge—it was a mere arch, with a vault
underneath that looked temptingly sheltered and cosy to
wearied eyes.

The dam was bare, and I had to pull off to the east,
on to the swampy plain. I gave my horses the lines, and
slowly, slowly they took me home! Even had I not
always lost interest here, to-day I should have leaned
back and rested. Although the horses had done all the
actual work, the strain of it had been largely on me. It
was the after-effect that set in now.

I thought of my wife, and of how she would have
felt had she been able to follow the scenes in some magi-
cal mirror through every single vicissitude of my drive.
And once more I saw with the eye of recent memory the
horses in that long, endless plunge through the corner
of the marsh. Once more I felt my muscles a-quiver with
the strain of that last wild struggle over that last, inhuman drift. And slowly I made up my mind that the
next time, the very next day, on my return trip, I was
going to add another eleven miles to my already long
drive and to take a different road. I knew the trail over
which I had been coming so far was closed for the rest
of the winter—there was no traffic there—no trail would
be kept open. That other road of which I was thinking
and which lay further west was the main cordwood trail
to the towns in the south. It was out of my way, to be
sure, but I felt convinced that I could spare my horses
and even save time by making the detour.

Being on the east side of the dam, I could not see

school or cottage till I turned up on the correction line.
But when at last I saw it, I felt somewhat as I had felt
coming home from my first big trip overseas. It seemed
a lifetime since I had started out. I seemed to be a different man.

Here, in the timber land, the snow had not drifted to
any extent. There were signs of the gale, but its record
was written in fallen tree trunks, broken branches, a
litter of twigs—not in drifts of snow. My wife would not
surmise what I had gone through.

She came out with a smile on her face when I pulled
in on the yard. It was characteristic of her that she did
not ask why I came so late; she accepted the fact as
something for which there were no doubt compelling
reasons. "I was giving our girl a bath," she said; "she
cannot come." And then she looked wistfully at my face
and at the horses. Silently I slipped the harness off their
backs. I used to let them have their freedom for a while
on reaching home. And never yet but Peter at least had
had a kick and a caper and a roll before they sought
their mangers. To-day they stood for a moment knock-
kneed, without moving, then shook themselves in a
weak, half-hearted way and went with drooping heads
and weary limbs straight to the stable.

"You had a hard trip?" asked my wife; and I replied
with as much cheer as I could muster, "I have seen sights
to-day that I did not expect to see before my dying day."
And taking her arm, I looked at the westering sun and
turned towards the house.

Chapter 5

WIND AND WAVES

WHEN I awoke on the morning after the last described arrival at "home," I thought of the angry glow in the east at sunrise of the day before. It had been cold again over night, so cold that in the small cottage, whatever was capable of freezing, froze to its very core. The frost had even penetrated the hole which in this "teacher's residence" made shift for a cellar, and, in spite of their being covered with layer upon layer of empty bags, had sweetened the winter's supply of potatoes.

But towards morning there had been a let-up, a sudden rise in temperature, as we experience it so often, coincident with a change in the direction of the wind, which now blew rather briskly from the south, foreboding a storm.

I got the horses ready at an early hour, for I was going to try the roundabout way at last, forty-five miles of it; and never before had I gone over the whole of it in winter. Even in summer I had done so only once, and that in a car, when I had accompanied the schoolinspector on one of his trips. I wanted to make sure that I should be ready in time to start at ten o'clock in the morning.

This new road had chiefly two features which recommended it to me. Firstly, about thirty-eight miles out of forty-five led through a fairly well settled district where I could hope to find a chain of short-haul trails. The widest gap in this series of settlements was one of two miles where there was wild land. The remaining seven miles, it is true, led across that wilderness on the east side of which lay Bell's farm. This piece, however, I

knew so well that I felt sure of finding my way there by
night or day in any reasonable kind of weather. Nor did
I expect to find it badly drifted. And secondly, about
twenty-nine miles from "home" I should pass within one
mile of a town which boasted of boarding house and
livery stable, offering thus, in case of an emergency, a
convenient stopping place.

I watched the sky rather anxiously, not so much on
my own account as because my wife, seeing me start,
would worry a good deal should that start be made in
foul weather. At nine the sky began to get grey in spots.
Shortly after a big cloud came sailing up, and I went out
to watch it. And sure enough, it had that altogether loose
appearance, with those wind-torn, cottony appendages
hanging down from its darker upper body which are
sure to bring snow. Lower away in the south—a rare
thing to come from the south in our climate—there lay
a black squall-cloud with a rounded outline, like a big
windbag, resembling nothing so much as a fat boy's face
with its cheeks blown out, when he tries to fill a football
with the pressure from his lungs. That was an infallible
sign. The first cloud, which was travelling fast, might
blow over. The second, larger one was sure to bring wind
a-plenty. But still there was hope. So long as it did not
bring outright snow, my wife would not worry so much.
Here where she was, the snow would not drift—there was
altogether too much bush. She—not having been much
of an observer of the skies before—dreaded the snowstorm more than the blizzard. I knew the latter was what
portended danger.

When I turned back into the house, a new thought
struck me. I spoke to my wife, who was putting up a
lunch for me, and proposed to take her and our little girl
over to a neighbour's place a mile and a half west of the
school. Those people were among the very few who had
been decent to her, and the visit would beguile the weary

Sunday afternoon. She agreed at once. So we all got ready; I brought the horses out and hooked them up, alone—no trouble from them this morning: they were quiet enough when they drank deep at the well.

A few whirls of snow had come down meanwhile—not enough, however, as yet to show as a new layer on the older snow. Again a cloud had torn loose from that squall-bag on the horizon, and again it showed that cottony, fringy, whitish under-layer which meant snow. I raised the top of the cutter and fastened the curtains.

By the time we three piled in, the thin flakes were dancing all around again, dusting our furs with their thin, glittering crystals. I bandied baby-talk with the little girl to make things look cheerful, but there was anguish in the young woman's look. I saw she would like to ask me to stay over till Monday, but she knew that I considered it my duty to get back to town by night.

The short drive to the neighbour's place was pleasant enough. There was plenty of snow on this part of the correction line, which farther east was bare; and it was packed down by abundant traffic. Then came the parting. I kissed wife and child; and slowly, accompanied by much waving of hands on the part of the little girl and a rather depressed-looking smile on that of my wife, I turned on the yard and swung back to the road. The cliffs of black poplar boles engulfed me at once: a sheltered grade.

But I had not yet gone very far—a mile perhaps, or a little over—when the trees began to bend under the impact of that squall. Nearly at the same moment the sun, which so far had been shining in an intermittent way, was blotted from the sky, and it turned almost dusky. For a long while—for more than an hour, indeed—it had seemed as if that black squall-cloud were lying motionless at the horizon—an anchored ship, bulging at its wharf. But then, as if its moorings had been cast off,

or its sails unfurled, it travelled up with amazing speed.
The wind had an easterly slant to it—a rare thing with
us for a wind from that quarter to bring a heavy storm.
The gale had hardly been blowing for ten or fifteen
minutes, when the snow began to whirl down. It came in
the tiniest possible flakes, consisting this time of short
needles that looked like miniature spindles, strung with
the smallest imaginable globules of ice—no six-armed
crystals that I could find so far. Many a snowstorm begins that way with us. And there was even here, in the
chasm of the road, a swing and dance to the flakes that
bespoke the force of the wind above.

My total direction—after I should have turned off
the correction line—lay to the southeast, into the very
teeth of the wind. I had to make it by laps though, first
south, then east, then south again, with the exception of
six or seven miles across the wild land west of Bell's
corner; there, as nearly as I could hold the direction, I
should have to strike a true line southeast.

I timed my horses; I could not possibly urge them
on to-day. They took about nine minutes to the mile, and
I knew I should have to give them many a walk. That
meant at best a drive of eight hours. It would be dark
before I reached town. I did not mind that, for I knew
there would be many a night drive ahead, and I felt sure
that that half-mile on the southern correction line, one
mile from town, would have been gone over on Saturday
by quite a number of teams. The snow settles down considerably, too, in thirty hours, especially under the pressure of wind. If a trail had been made over the drift, I
was confident my horses would find it without fail. So I
dismissed all anxiety on my own score.

But all the more did the thought of my wife worry
me. If only I could have made her see things with my
own eyes—but I could not. She regarded me as an in-
valid whose health was undermined by a wasting illness

and who needed nursing and coddling on the slightest provocation. Instead of drawing Nature's inference that what cannot live, should die, she clung to the slender thread of life that sometimes threatened to break—but never on these drives. I often told her that, if I could make my living by driving instead of teaching, I should feel the stronger, the healthier, and the better for it—my main problem would have been solved. But she, with a woman's instinct for shelter and home, cowered down before every one of Nature's menaces. And yet she bore up with remarkable courage.

A mile or so before I came to the turn in my road the forest withdrew on both sides, yielding space to the fields and elbow-room for the wind to unfold its wings. As soon as its full force struck the cutter, the curtains began to emit that crackling sound which indicates to the sailor that he has turned his craft as far into the wind as he can safely do without losing speed. Little ripples ran through the bulging canvas. As yet I sat snug and sheltered within, my left shoulder turned to the weather, but soon I sighted dimly a curtain of trees that ran at right angles to my road. Behind it there stood a school building, and beyond that I should have to turn south. I gave the horses a walk. I decided to give them a walk of five minutes for every hour they trotted along. We reached the corner that way, and I started them up again.

Instantly things changed. We met the wind at an angle of about thirty degrees from the southeast. The air looked thick ahead. I moved into the left-hand corner of the seat, and though the full force of the wind did not strike me there, the whirling snow did not respect my shelter. It blew in slantways under the top, then described a curve upward, and downward again, as if it were going to settle on the right end of the back. But just before it touched the back, it turned at a sharp angle and piled on to my right side. A fair proportion of it reached my face which soon became wet and then caked over with ice. There was a sting to the flakes which made them rather disagreeable. My right eye kept closing up, and I had to wipe it often to keep it open. The wind, too, for the first and only time on my drives, somehow found an entrance into the lower part of the cutter box, and though my feet were resting on the heater and my legs were wrapped, first in woollen and then in leather leggings, besides being covered with a good fur robe, my left side soon began to feel the cold. It may be that this comparative discomfort, which I had to endure for the better part of the day, somewhat coloured the kind of experience this drive became.

As far as the road was concerned, I had as yet little to complain of. About three miles from the turn there stood a Lutheran church frequented by the Russian Germans that formed a settlement for miles around. They had made the trail for me on these three miles, and even for a matter of four or five miles south of the church, as I found out. It is that kind of a road which you want for long drives: where others who have short drives and, therefore, do not need to consider their horses break the crust of the snow and pack it down. I hoped that a goodly part of my day's trip would be in the nature of a chain of shorter, much frequented stretches; and on the whole I was not to be disappointed.

Doubtless all my readers know how a country road that is covered with from two to three feet of snow will look when the trail is broken. There is a smooth expanse, mostly somewhat hardened at the surface, and there are two deep-cut tracks in it, each about ten to twelve inches wide, sharply defined, with the snow at the bottom packed down by the horses' feet and the runners of the respective conveyances. So long as you have such a trail and horses with road sense, you do not need to worry about your directions, no matter how badly it may blow.

Horses that are used to travelling in the snow will never leave the trail, for they dread nothing so much as breaking in on the sides. This fact released my attention for other things.

Now I thought again for a while of home, of how my wife would be worrying, how even the little girl would be infected by her nervousness—how she would ask, "Mamma, is Daddy in . . . now?" But I did not care to follow up these thoughts too far. They made me feel too soft.

After that I just sat there for a while and looked ahead. But I saw only the whirl, whirl, whirl of the snow slanting across my field of vision. You are closed in by it as by insecure and ever receding walls when you drive in a snowstorm. If I had met a team, I could not have seen it, and if my safety had depended on my discerning it in time to turn out of the road, my safety would not have been very safe indeed. But I could rely on my horses: they would hear the bells of any encountering conveyance long enough ahead to betray it to me by their behaviour. And should I not even notice that, they would turn out in time of their own accord: they had a great deal of road sense.

Weariness overcame me. In the open the howling and whistling of the wind always acts on me like a soporific. Inside of a house it is just the reverse; I know nothing that will keep my nerves as much on edge and prevent me as certainly from sleeping as the voices at night of a gale around the buildings. I needed something more definite to look at than that prospect ahead. The snow was by this time piling in on the seat at my right and in the box, so as to exclude all draughts except from below. I felt that as a distinct advantage.

Without any conscious intention I began to peer out below the slanting edge of the left side-curtain and to watch the sharp crest-wave of snow-spray thrown by the

curve of the runner where it cut into the freshly accumu-
lating mass. It looked like the wing-wave thrown to
either side by the bow of a power boat that cuts swiftly
through quiet water. From it my eye began to slip over
to the snow expanse. The road was wide, lined with
brush along the fence to the left. The fields beyond had
no very large open areas—windbreaks had everywhere
been spared out when the primeval forest had first been
broken into by the early settlers. So whatever the force
of the wind might be, no high drift layer could form. But
still the snow drifted. There was enough coming down
from above to supply material even on such a narrow
strip as a road allowance. It was the manner of this drifting that held my eye and my attention at last.

All this is, of course, utterly trivial. I had observed it
myself a hundred times before. I observe it again to-day
at this very writing, in the first blizzard of the season.
It always has a strange fascination for me; but maybe I
need to apologize for setting it down in writing.

The wind would send the snowflakes at a sharp angle
downward to the older surface. There was no impact,
as there is with rain. The flakes, of course, did not re-
bound. But they did not come to rest either, not for the
most imperceptible fraction of time. As soon as they
touched the white, underlying surface, they would start
to scud along horizontally at a most amazing speed,
forming with their previous path an obtuse angle. So
long as I watched the single flake—which is quite a task,
especially while driving—it seemed to be in a tremendous hurry. It rushed along very nearly at the speed of
the wind, and that was considerable, say between thirty-
five and forty miles an hour or even more. But then,
when it hit the trail, the track made by horses and runners, strange to say, it did not fall down perpendicularly,
as it would have done had it acted there under the influence of gravity alone; but it started on a curved path

towards the lower edge of the opposite wall of the track
and there, without touching the wall, it started back, first
downward, thus making the turn, and then upward
again, towards the upper edge of the east wall, and not
in a straight line either, but in a wavy curve, rising very
nearly but not quite to the edge; and only then would it
settle down against the eastern wall of the track, helping
to fill it in. I watched this with all the utmost effort of
attention of which I was capable. I became intensely
interested in my observations. I even made sure—as sure
as anybody can be of anything—that the whole of this
curious path lay in the same perpendicular plane which
ran from the southeast to the northwest, that is to say in
the direction of the main current of the wind. I have
since confirmed these observations many times.

I am aware of the fact that nobody—nobody whom I
know, at least—takes the slightest interest in such things.
People watch birds because some "Nature-Study
cranks" (I am one of them) urge it in the schools. Others
will make desultory observations on "Weeds" or
"Native Trees." Our school work in this respect seems
to me to be most ridiculously and palpably superficial.
Worst of all, most of it is dry as dust, and it leads nowhere. I sometimes fear there is something wrong with
my own mentality. But to me it seems that the Kingdom
of Heaven lies all around us, and that most of us simply
prefer the moving-picture show. I have kept weather
records for whole seasons—brief notes on the everyday
observations of mere nothings. You, for whom above all
I am setting these things down, will find them among my
papers one day. They would seem meaningless to most
of my fellowmen, I believe; to me they are absorbingly
interesting reading when once in a great while I pick an
older record up and glance it over. But this is digressing.

Now slowly, slowly another fact came home to me.
This unanimous, synchronous march of all the flakes

coming down over hundreds of square miles—and I was watching it myself over miles upon miles of road—in spite of the fact that every single flake seemed to be in the greatest possible hurry—was, judged as a whole, nevertheless an exceedingly leisurely process. In one respect it reminded me of bees swarming; watch the single bee, and it seems to fly at its utmost speed; watch the swarm, and it seems to be merely floating along. The reason, of course, is entirely different. The bees wheel and circle around individually, the whole swarm revolves —if I remember right, Burroughs has well described it (as what has he not?).* But the snow will not change its direction while drifting in a wind that blows straight ahead. Its direction is from first to last the resultant of the direction of the wind and that of the pull of gravity, into which there enters besides only the ratio of the strengths of these two forces. The single snowflake is to the indifferent eye something infinitesimal, too small to take individual notice of, once it reaches the ground. For most of us it hardly has any separate existence, however it may be to more astute observers. We see the flakes in the mass, and we judge by results. Now firstly, to talk of results, the filling up of a hollow, unless the drifting snow is simply picked up from the ground where it lay ready from previous falls, proceeds itself rather slowly and in quite a leisurely way. But secondly, and this is the more important reason, the snow moves in waves of greater and lesser density; these waves—and I do not know whether this observation has ever been recorded though doubtless it has been made by better observers than I am—these waves, I say, are propagated in a direction opposite to that of the wind. They are like soundwaves sent into the teeth of the wind, only they travel more slowly. Anybody who has observed a really splashing

* Yes; I looked it up. See the "Pastoral Bees" in *Locusts and Wild Honey*.

rain on smooth ground—on a cement sidewalk, for instance—must have observed that the rebounding drops, like those that are falling, form streaks, because they, too, are arranged in vertical layers—or sheets—of greater and lesser density—or maybe the term "frequency" would be more appropriate; and these streaks travel as compared with the wind, and, as compared with its direction, they travel against it. It is this that causes the curious criss-cross pattern of falling and rebounding rain-streaks in heavy showers. Quite likely there are more competent observers who might analyse these phenomena better than I can do it; but if nobody else does, maybe I shall one day make public a little volume containing observations on our summer rains. But again I am digressing.

The snow, then, hits the surface of the older layers in waves, no matter whether the snow is freshly falling or merely drifting; and it is these waves that you notice most distinctly. Although they travel with the wind when you compare their position with points on the ground—yet, when compared with the rushing air above, it becomes clear that they travel against it. The waves, I say, not the flakes. The single flake never stops in its career, except as it may be retarded by friction and other resistances. But the aggregation of the multitudes of flakes, which varies constantly in its substance, creates the impression as if the snow travelled very much more slowly than in reality it does. In other words, every single flake, carried on by inertia, constantly passes from one air wave to the next one, but the waves themselves remain relatively stationary. They swing along in undulating, comparatively slow-moving sheets which may simply be retarded behind the speed of the wind, but more probably form an actual reaction, set up by a positive force counteracting the wind, whatever its origin may be.

When at last I had fully satisfied my mind as to the

somewhat complicated mechanics of this thing, I settled
back in my seat—against a cushion of snow that had
meanwhile piled in behind my spine. If I remember
right, I had by this time well passed the church. But for
a while longer I looked out through the triangular opening between the door of the cutter and the curtain. I did
not watch snowflakes or waves any longer, but I matured
an impression. At last it ripened into words.

Yes, the snow, as figured in the waves, *crawled* over
the ground. There was in the image that engraved itself
on my memory something cruel—I could not help thinking of the "cruel, crawling foam" and the ruminating
pedant Ruskin, and I laughed. "The cruel, crawling
snow!" Yes, and in spite of Ruskin and his "pathetic
fallacy," there it was! Of course, the snow is not cruel.
Of course, it merely is propelled by something which,
according to Karl Pearson, I do not even with a good
scientific conscience dare to call a "force" any longer.
But nevertheless, it made the impression of cruelty, and
in that lay its fascination and beauty. It even reminded
me of a cat slowly reaching out with armed claw for the
"innocent" bird. But the cat is not cruel either—we
merely call it so! Oh, for the juggling of words! . . .

Suddenly my horses brought up on a farmyard. They
had followed the last of the church-goers' trails, had not
seen any other trail ahead and had faithfully done their
horse-duty by staying on what they considered to be the
road.

I had reached the northern limit of that two-mile
stretch of wild land. In summer there is a distinct and
good road here, but for the present the snow had engulfed it. When I had turned back to the bend of the
trail, I was for the first time up against a small fraction
of what was to come. No trail, and no possibility of tell-
ing the direction in which I was going! Fortunately I
realized the difficulty right from the start. Before setting

out, I looked back to the farm and took my bearings from the fence of the front yard which ran north-south. Then I tried to hold to the line thus gained as best I could. It was by no means an easy matter, for I had to wind my weary way around old and new drifts, brush and trees. The horses were mostly up to their knees in snow, carefully lifting their hindlegs to place them in the cavities which their forelegs made. Occasionally, much as I tried to avoid it, I had to make a short dash through a snow dam thrown up over brush that seemed to encircle me completely. The going, to be sure, was not so heavy as it had been the day before on the corner of the marsh, but on the other hand I could not see as far beyond the horses' heads. And had I been able to see, the less conspicuous landmarks would not have helped me since I did not know them. It took us about an hour to cross this untilled and unfenced strip. I came out on the next crossroad, not more than two hundred yards east of where I should have come out. I considered that excellent; but I soon was to understand that it was owing only to the fact that so far I had had no flying drifts to go through. Up to this point the snow was "crawling" only wherever the thicket opened up a little. What blinded my vision had so far been only the new, falling snow.

I am sure I looked like a snowman. Whenever I shook my big gauntlets bare, a cloud of exceedingly fine and hard snow crystals would hit my face; and seeing how much I still had ahead, I cannot say that I liked the sensation. I was getting thoroughly chilled by this time. The mercury probably stood at somewhere between minus ten and twenty. The very next week I made one trip at forty below—a thermometer which I saw and the accuracy of which I have no reason to doubt showed minus forty-eight degrees. Anyway, it was the coldest night of the winter, but I was not to suffer then. I remem-

ber how about five in the morning, when I neared the
northern correction line, my lips began to stiffen; hard,
frozen patches formed on my cheeks, and I had to allow
the horses to rub their noses on fence posts or trees every
now and then, to knock the big icicles off and to prevent
them from freezing up altogether—but my feet and my
hands and my body kept warm, for there was no wind.
On drives like these your well-being depends largely on
the state of your feet and hands. But on this return trip
I surely did suffer. Every now and then my fingers would
turn curd-white, and I had to remove my gauntlets and
gloves, and to thrust my hands under my wraps, next to
my body. I also froze two toes rather badly. And what I
remember as particularly disagreeable, was that somehow my scalp got chilled. Slowly, slowly the wind
seemed to burrow its way under my fur cap and into my
hair. After a while it became impossible for me to move
scalp or brows. One side of my face was now thickly
caked over with ice—which protected, but also on
account of its stiffness caused a minor discomfort. So
far, however, I had managed to keep both my eyes at
work. And for a short while I needed them just now.

We were crossing a drift which had apparently not
been broken into since it had first been piled up the previous week. Such drifts are dangerous because they will
bear up for a while under the horses' weight, and then
the hard-pressed crust will break and reveal a softer core
inside. Just that happened here, and exactly at a
moment, too, when the drifting snow caught me with its
full force and at its full height. It was a quarter-minute
of stumbling, jumping, pulling one against the other—
and then a rally, and we emerged in front of a farmyard
from which a fairly fresh trail led south. This trail was
filled in, it is true, for the wind here pitched the snow by
the shovelful, but the difference in colour between the
pure white, new snow that filled it and the older surface

to both sides made it sufficiently distinct for the horses to follow. They plodded along.

Here miles upon miles of open fields lay to the southeast, and the snow that fell over all these fields was at once picked up by the wind and started its irresistible march to the northwest. And no longer did it crawl. Since it was bound upon a long-distance trip, somewhere in its career it would be caught in an upward sweep of the wind and thrown aloft, and then it would hurtle along at the speed of the wind, blotting everything from sight, hitting hard whatever it encountered, and piling in wherever it found a sheltered space. The height of this drifting snow layer varies, of course, directly and jointly (here the teacher makes fun of his mathematics) as the amount of loose snow available and as the carrying force of the wind. Many, many years ago I once saved the day by climbing on to the seat of my cutter and looking around from this vantage-point. I was lost and had no idea of where I was. There was no snowstorm going on at the time, but a recent snowfall was being driven along by a merciless northern gale. As soon as I stood erect on my seat, my head reached into a less dense drift layer, and I could clearly discern a farmhouse not more than a few hundred yards away. I had been on the point of accepting it as a fact that I was lost. Those tactics would not have done on this particular day, there being the snowstorm to reckon with. For the moment, not being lost, I was in no need of them, anyway. But even later the possible but doubtful advantage to be gained by them seemed more than offset by the great and certain disadvantage of having to get out of my robes and to expose myself to the chilling wind.

This north-south road was in the future invariably to seem endlessly long to me. There were no very prominent landmarks—a school somewhere—and there was hardly any change in the monotony of driving. As for landmarks, I should mention that there was one more at least. About two miles from the turn into that town which I have mentioned I crossed a bridge, and beyond this bridge the trail sloped sharply up in an S-shaped curve to a level about twenty or twenty-five feet higher than that of the road along which I had been driving. The bridge had a rail on its west side; but the other rail had been broken down in some accident and had never been replaced. I mention this trifle because it became important in an incident during the last drive which I am going to describe.

On we went. We passed the school, of which I did not see much except the flagpole. And then we came to the crossroads where the trail bent west into the town. If I had known the road more thoroughly, I should have turned there, too. It would have added another two miles to my already overlong trip, but I invariably did it later on. Firstly, the horses will rest up much more completely when put into a stable for feeding. And secondly, there always radiate from a town fairly well beaten trails. It is a mistake to cut across from one such trail to another. The straight road, though much shorter, is apt to be entirely untravelled, and to break trail after a heavy snowstorm is about as hard a task as any that you can put your team up against. I had the road; there was no mistaking it; it ran along between trees and fences which were plainly visible; but there were ditches and brush buried under the snow which covered the grade to a depth of maybe three feet, and every bit of these drifts was of that treacherous character that I have described.

If you look at some small drift piled up against the glass pane of a storm window, you can plainly see how the snow, even in such a miniature pile, preserves the stratified appearance which is the consequence of its being laid down in layers of varying density. Now after

it has been lying for some time, it will form a crust on
top which is sometimes the effect of wind pressure and
sometimes—under favourable conditions—of superficial glaciation. A similar condensation takes place at the
bottom as the result of the work of gravity: a harder core
will form. Between the two there is layer upon layer of
comparatively softer snow. In these softer layers the
differences which are due to the stratified precipitation
still remain. And frequently they will make the going
particularly uncertain; for a horse will break through in
stages only. He thinks that he has reached the carrying
stratum, gets ready to take his next step—thereby throwing his whole weight on two or at best three feet—and
just when he is off his balance, there is another caving in.
I believe it is this that makes horses so nervous when
crossing drifts. Later on in the winter there is, of course,
the additional complication of successive snowfalls. The
layers from this cause are usually clearly discernible by
differences in colour.

I have never figured out just how far I went along this
entirely unbroken road, but I believe it must have been
for two miles. I know that my horses were pretty well
spent by the time we hit upon another trail. It goes without saying that this trail, too, though it came from town,
had not been gone over during the day and therefore
consisted of nothing but a pair of whiter ribbons on the
drifts; but underneath these ribbons the snow was
packed. Hardly anybody cares to be out on a day like
that, not even for a short drive. And though in this
respect I differ in my tastes from other people, provided
I can keep myself from actually getting chilled, even I
began to feel rather forlorn, and that is saying a good
deal.

A few hundred yards beyond the point where we had
hit upon this new trail which was only faintly visible,
the horses turned eastward, on to a field. Between two

posts the wire of the fence had been taken down, and
since I could not see any trail leading along the road
further south, I let my horses have their will. I knew
the farm on which we were. It was famous all around
for its splendid, pure-bred beef cattle herd. I had not
counted on crossing it, but I knew that after a mile of
this field trail I should emerge on the farmyard, and
since I was particularly well acquainted with the trail
from there across the wild land to Bell's corner, it suited
me to do as my horses suggested. As a matter of fact this
trail became—with the exception of one drive—my
regular route for the rest of the winter. Never again was
I to meet with the slightest mishap on this particular run.
But to-day I was to come as near getting lost as I ever
came during the winter, on those drives to and from the
north.

For the next ten minutes I watched the work of the
wind on the open field. As is always the case with me,
I was not content with recording a mere observation. I
had watched the thing a hundred times before. "Observing" means to me as much finding words to express what
I see as it means the seeing itself. Now, when a house-
wife takes a thin sheet that is lying on the bed and shakes
it up without changing its horizontal position, the running waves of air caught under the cloth will throw it
into a motion very similar to that which the wind imparts
to the snow-sheets, only that the snow-sheets will run
down instead of up. Under a good head of wind there is
a vehemence in this motion that suggests anger and a
violent disposition. The sheets of snow are "flapped"
down. Then suddenly the direction of the wind changes
slightly, and the sheet is no longer flapped down but
blown up. At the line where the two motions join we
have that edge the appearance of which suggested to me
the comparison with "exfoliated" rock in a previous
place. It is for this particular stage in the process of

bringing about that appearance that I tentatively proposed the term "adfoliation." "Adfoliated" edges are always to be found on the lee side of the sheet.

Sometimes, however, the opposite process will bring about nearly the same result. The snow-sheet has been spread, and a downward sweep of violent wind will hit the surface, denting it, scraping away an edge of the top layer, and usually gripping through into lower layers; then, rebounding, it will lift the whole sheet up again, or any part of it; and, shattering it into its component crystals, will throw these aloft and afar to be laid down again further on. This is true "exfoliation." Since it takes a more violent burst of wind to effect this true exfoliation than it does to bring about the adfoliation, and since, further, the snow, once indented, will yield to the depth of several layers, the true exfoliation edges are usually thicker than the others: and, of course, they are always to be found on the wind side.

Both kinds of lines are wavy lines because the sheets of wind are undulating. In this connection I might repeat once more that the straight line seems to be quite unknown in Nature, as also is uniformity of motion. I once watched very carefully a ferry cable strung across the bottom of a mighty river, and, failing to discover any theoretical reason for its vibratory motion, I was thrown back upon proving to my own satisfaction that the motion even of that flowing water in the river was the motion of a pulse; and I still believe that my experiments were conclusive. Everybody, of course, is familiar with the vibrations of telephone wires in a breeze. That humming sound which they emit would indeed be hard to explain without the assumption of a pulsating blow. Of course, it is easy to prove this pulsation in air. From certain further observations, which I do not care to speak about at present, I am inclined to assume a pulsating arrangement, or an alternation of layers of greater and lesser density in all organised—that is, crystalline—matter; for instance, in even such an apparently uniform block as a lump of metallic gold or copper or iron. This arrangement, of course, may be disturbed by artificial means; but if it is, the matter seems to be in an unstable condition, as is proved, for instance, by the sudden, unexpected breaking of apparently perfectly sound steel rails. There seems to be a condition of matter which so far we have largely failed to take into account or to utilise in human affairs. . . .

I reached the yard, crossed it, and swung out through the front gate. Nowhere was anybody to be seen. The yard itself is sheltered by a curtain of splendid wild trees to the north, the east, and the south. So I had a breathing spell for a few minutes. I could also clearly see the gap in this windbreak through which I must reach the open. I think I mentioned that on the previous drive, going north, I had found the road four or five miles east of here very good indeed. But the reason had been that just this windbreak, which angles over to what I have been calling the twelve-mile bridge, prevented all serious drifting while the wind came from the north. To-day I was to find things different, for to the south the land was altogether open. The force of the wind alone was sufficient to pull the horses back to a walk, before we even had quite reached the open plain. It was a little after four when I crossed the gap, and I knew that I should have to make the greater part of what remained in darkness. I was about twelve miles from town, I should judge. The horses had not been fed. So, as soon as I saw how things were, I turned back into the shelter of the bluff to feed. I might have gone to the farm, but I was afraid it would cost too much time. After this I always went into town and fed in the stable. While the horses were eating and resting, I cleaned the cutter of snow, looked after my footwarmer, and, by tramping about

and kicking against the tree trunks, tried to get my be-
numbed circulation started again. My own lunch on
examination proved to be frozen into one hard, solid
lump. So I decided to go without it and to save it for my
supper.

At half past four we crossed the gap in the bluffs for
the second time.

Words fail me to describe or even to suggest the fury
of the blast and of the drift into which we emerged. For
a moment I thought the top of the cutter would be blown
off. With the twilight that had set in, the wind had in-
creased to a baffling degree. The horses came as near
as they ever came, in any weather, to turning on me and
refusing to face the gale. And what with my blurred
vision, the twisting and dodging about of the horses, and
the gathering dusk, I soon did not know any longer
where I was. There was ample opportunity to go wrong.
Copses, single trees, and burnt stumps which dotted the
wilderness had a knack of looming up with startling
suddenness in front or on the side, sometimes dangerously
close to the cutter. It was impossible to look straight
ahead, because the ice crystals which mimicked snow
cut right into my eyes and made my lids smart with sore-
ness. Underfoot the rough ground seemed like a heaving
sea. The horses would stumble, and the cutter would
pitch over from one side to the other in the most alarming way. I saw no remedy. It was useless to try to avoid
the obstacles—only once did I do so, and that time I had
to back away from a high stump against which my drawbar had brought up. The pitching and rolling of the
cutter repeatedly shook me out of my robes, and if, when
starting up again from the bluff, I had felt a trifle more
comfortable, that increment of consolation was soon
lost.

We wallowed about—there is only this word to suggest the motion. To all intents and purposes I was lost.

But still there was one thing, provided it had not changed, to tell me the approximate direction—the wind. It had been coming from the south-southeast. So, by driving along very nearly into its teeth, I could, so I thought, not help emerging on the road to town.

Repeatedly I wished I had taken the old trail. That fearful drift in the bush beyond the creek, I thought, surely had settled down somewhat in twenty-four hours.* I had had as much or more of unbroken trail to-day as on the day before. On the whole, though, I still believed that the four miles across the corner of the marsh south of the creek had been without a parallel in their demands on the horses' endurance. And gradually I came to see that after all the horses probably would have given out before this, under the cumulative effect of two days of it, had they not found things somewhat more endurable to-day.

We wallowed along. . . . And then we stopped. I shouted to the horses—nothing but a shout could have the slightest effect against the wind. They started to fidget and to dance and to turn this way and that, but they would not go. I wasted three or four minutes before I shook free of my robes and jumped out to investigate. Well, we were in the corner formed by two fences— caught as in a trap. I was dumbfounded. I did not know of any fence in these parts—none where I thought I should be. And how had we got into it? I had not passed through any gate. There was, of course, no use in conjecturing. If the wind had not veered around completely, one of the fences must run north-south, the other one east-west, and we were in the southeast corner of some farm. Where there was a fence, I was likely to find a

* As a matter of fact I was to see it once more before the winter was over, and I found it settled down to about one-third its original height. This was partly the result of superficial thawing. But even then, shortly before the final thaw-up, it still looked formidable enough.

farmyard. It could not be to the east, so there remained three guesses. I turned back to the west. I skirted the fence closely, so closely that even in the failing light and in spite of the drifting snow I did not lose sight of it. Soon the going began to be less rough; the choppy motion of the cutter semed to indicate that we were on fall-ploughed land; and not much later Peter gave a snort. We were apparently nearing a group of buildings. I heard the heavy thump of galloping horses, and a second later I saw a light which moved.

I hailed the man; and he came over and answered my questions. Yes, the wind had turned somewhat; it came nearly from the east now (so that was what had misled me); I was only half a mile west of my old trail, but still, for all that, nearly twelve miles from town. In this there was good news as well as bad. I remembered the place now; just south of the twelve-mile bridge I had often caught sight of it to the west. Instead of crossing the wild land along its diagonal, I had, deceived by the changed direction of the wind, skirted its northern edge, holding close to the line of poplars. I thought of the fence: yes, the man who answered my questions was renting from the owner of that pure-bred Angus herd; he was hauling wood for him and had taken the fence on the west side down. I had passed between two posts without noticing them. He showed me the south gate and gave me the general direction. He even offered my horses water, which they drank eagerly enough. But he did not offer bed and stable-room for the night; nor did he open the gate for me, as I had hoped he would. I should have declined the night's accommodation, but I should have been grateful for a helping hand at the gate. I had to get out of my wraps to open it. And meanwhile I had been getting out and in so often, that I did no longer even care to clean my feet of snow; I simply pushed the heater aside so as to prevent it from melting.

I "bundled in"—that word, borrowed from an angry lady, describes my mood perhaps better than anything else I might say. And yet, though what followed was not exactly pleasure, my troubles were over for the day. The horses, of course, still had a weary, weary time of it, but as soon as we got back to our old trail—which we presently did—they knew the road at least. I saw that the very moment we reached it by the way they turned on to it and stepped out more briskly.

From this point on we had about eleven miles to make, and every step of it was made at a walk. I cannot, of course, say much about the road. There was nothing for me to do except as best I could to fight the wind. I got my tarpaulin out from under the seat and spread it over myself. I verily believe I nodded repeatedly. It did not matter. I knew that the horses would take me home, and since it was absolutely dark, I could not have helped it had they lost their way. A few times, thinking that I noticed an improvement in the road, I tried to speed the horses up; but when Dan at last, in an attempt to respond, went down on his knees, I gave it up. Sometimes we pitched and rolled again for a space, but mostly things went quietly enough. The wind made a curious sound, something between an infuriated whistle and the sibilant noise a man makes when he draws his breath in sharply between his teeth.

I do not know how long we may have been going that way. But I remember how at last suddenly and gradually I realized that there was a change in our motion. Suddenly, I say—for the realization of the change came as a surprise; probably I had been nodding, and I started up. Gradually—for I believe it took me quite an appreciable time before I awoke to the fact that the horses at last were trotting. It was a weary, slow, jogging trot—but it electrified me, for I knew at once that we were on our very last mile. I strained my eye-sight, but I could see no light ahead. In fact, we were crossing the bridge before I saw the first light of the town.

The livery stable was deserted. I had to open the doors, to drive in, to unhitch, to unharness, and to feed the horses myself. And then I went home to my cold and lonesome house.

It was a cheerless night.

Chapter 6

A CALL FOR SPEED

I HELD the horses in at the start. Somehow they realized that a new kind of test was ahead. They caught the infection of speed from my voice, I suppose, or from my impatience. They had not been harnessed by the hostler either. When I came to the stable—it was in the forenoon, too, at an hour when they had never been taken out before—the hostler had been away hauling feed. The boys whom I had pressed into service had pulled the cutter out into the street; it was there we hitched up. Everything, then, had been different from the way they had been used to. So, when at last I clicked my tongue, they bounded off as if they were out for a sprint of a few miles only.

I held them in and pulled them down to a trot; for of all days to-day was it of the utmost importance that neither one of them should play out. At half past twelve a telephone message had reached me, after having passed through three different channels, that my little girl was sick; and over the wire it had a sinister, lugubrious, reticent sound, as if the worst was held back. Details had not come through, so I was told. My wife was sending a call for me to come home as quickly as I possibly could; nothing else. It was Thursday. The Sunday before I had left wife and child in perfect health. But scarlatina and diphtheria were stalking the plains. The message had been such a shock to me that I had acted with automatic precision. I had notified the school board and asked the inspector to substitute for me; and twenty minutes after word had reached me I crossed the bridge on the road to the north.

The going was heavy but not too bad. Two nights ago there had been a rather bad snowstorm and a blow, and during the last night an exceedingly slight and quiet fall had followed it. Just now I had no eye for its beauty, though.

I was bent on speed, and that meant watching the horses closely; they must not be allowed to follow their own bent. There was no way of communicating with my wife; so that, whatever I could do, was left entirely to my divination. I had picked up a few things at the drug store—things which had occurred to me on the spur of the moment as likely to be needed; but now I started a process of analysis and elimination. Pneumonia, diphtheria, scarlatina and measles—all these were among the more obvious possibilities. I was enough of a doctor to trust my ability to diagnose. I knew that my wife would in that respect rather rely on me than on the average country-town practitioner. All the greater was my responsibility.

Since the horses had not been fed for their mid-day meal, I had in any case to put in at the one-third-way town. It had a drug store; so there was my last chance of getting what might possibly be needed. I made a list of remedies and rehearsed it mentally till I felt sure I should not omit anything of which I had thought.

Then I caught myself at driving the horses into a gallop. It was hard to hold in. I must confess that I thought but little of the little girl's side of it; more of my wife's; most of all of my own. That seems selfish. But ever since the little girl was born, there had been only one desire which filled my life. Where I had failed, she was to succeed. Where I had squandered my energies and opportunities, she was to use them to some purpose What I might have done but had not done, she was to do. She was to redeem me. I was her natural teacher Teaching her became henceforth my life-work. When I bought a book, I carefully considered whether it would help her one day or not before I spent the money. Deprived of her, I myself came to a definite and peremptory end. With her to continue my life, there was still some purpose in things, some justification for existence.

Most serious-minded men at my age, I believe, become profoundly impressed with the futility of "it all." Unless we throw ourselves into something outside of our own personality, life is apt to impress us as a great mockery. I am afraid that at the bottom of it there lies the recognition of the fact that we ourselves were not worth while, that we did not amount to what we had thought we should amount to; that we did not measure up to the exigencies of eternities to come. Children are among the most effective means devised by Nature to delude us into living on. Modern civilization has, on the whole, deprived us of the ability for the enjoyment of the moment. It raises our expectations too high—realization is bound to fall short, no matter what we do. We live in an artificial atmosphere. So we submerge ourselves in business, profession, or superficial amusement. We live for something—do not merely live. The wage-slave lives for the evening's liberty, the business man for his wealth, the preacher for his church. I used to live for my school. Then a moment like the one I was living through arrives. Nature strips down our pretences with a relentless finger, and we stand, bare of disguises, as helpless failures. We have lost the childlike power of living without conscious aims. Sometimes, when the aims have faded already in the gathering dusk, we still go on by the momentum acquired. Inertia carries us over the dead points—till a cog breaks somewhere, and our whole machinery of life comes to with a jar. If no such awakening supervenes, since we never live in the present, we are always looking forward to what never comes; and so life slips by, unlived.

If my child was taken from me, it meant that my future was made meaningless. I felt that I might just as well lie down and die.

There was injustice in this, I know. I was reasoning, as it were, in a phantom world. Actualities, outlooks, retrospections—my view of them had been jarred and distorted by an unexpected, stunning blow. For that it did not really matter how things actually were up north. I had never yet faced such possibilities; they opened up like an abyss which I had skirted in the dark, unknowingly. True, my wife was something like a child to me. I was old enough to be her father, older even in mind than in actual years. But she, too, by marrying an aging man, had limited her own development, as it were, by mine. Nor was she I, after all. My child was. The outlook without her was night. Such a life was not to be lived.

There was the lash of a scourge in these thoughts, so that I became nervous, impatient, and unjust—even to the horses. Peter stumbled, and I came near punishing him with my whip. But I caught myself just before I yielded to the impulse. I was doing exactly what I should not do. If Peter stumbled, it was more my own fault than his. I should have watched the road more carefully instead of giving in to the trend of my thoughts. A stumble every five minutes, and over a drive of forty-five miles: that might mean a delay of half an hour—it might mean the difference between "in time" and "too late." I did not know what waited at the other end of the road. It was my business to find out, not to indulge in mere surmises and forebodings.

So, with an effort, I forced my attention to revert to the things around. And Nature, with her utter lack of sentiment, is after all the only real soother of anguished nerves. With my mind in the state it was in, the drive would indeed have been nothing less than torture, had I

not felt, sometimes even against my will, mostly without
at any rate consciously yielding to it, the influence of
that merriest of all winter sights which surrounded me.

The fresh fall of snow, which had come over night,
was exceedingly slight. It had come down softly, float-
ingly, with all the winds of the prairies hushed, every
flake consisting of one or two large, flat crystals only,
which, on account of the nearly saturated air, had gone
on growing by condensation till they touched the
ground. Such a condition of the atmosphere never holds
out in a prolonged snowfall, may it come down ever so
soft-footedly; the first half hour exhausts the moisture
content of the air. After that the crystals are the ordinary,
small, six-armed "stars" which bunch together into
flakes. But if the snowfall is very slight, the moisture content of the lower air sometimes is not exhausted before
it stops; those large crystals remain at the surface and
are not buried out of sight by the later fall. These large,
coarse, slablike crystals reflect as well as refract the
light of the sun. There is not merely the sparkle and
glitter, but also the colour play. Facing north, you see
only glittering points of white light; but, facing the sun,
you see every colour of the rainbow, and you see it with
that coquettish, sudden flash which snow shares only
with the most precious of stones.

Through such a landscape covered with the thinnest
possible sheet of the white glitter we sped. A few times,
in heavier snow, the horses were inclined to fall into a
walk; but a touch of the whip sent them into line again.
I began to view the whole situation more quietly. Con-
sidering that we had forty-five miles to go, we were
doing very well indeed. We made Bell's corner in forty
minutes, and still I was saving the horses' strength.

On to the wild land we turned, where the snow underfoot was soft and free from those hard clods that cause
the horses' feet to stumble. I beguiled the time by watch-

ing the distance through the surrounding brush. Everybody, of course, has noticed how the open landscape seems to turn when you speed along. The distance seems to stand still, while the foreground rushes past you. The whole countryside seems to become a revolving, horizontal wheel with its hub at the horizon. It is different when you travel fast through half-open bush, so that the eye on its way to the edge of the visible world looks past trees and shrubs. In that case there are two points which speed along: you yourself, and with you, engaged, as it were, in a race with you, the distance. You can go many miles before your horizon changes. But between it and yourself the foreground is rushed back like a ribbon. There is no impression of wheeling; there is no depth to that ribbon which moves backward and past. You are also more distinctly aware that it is not the objects near you which move, but you yourself. Only a short distance from you trees and objects seem rather to move with you, though more slowly; and faster and faster all things seem to be moving in the same direction with you, the farther away they are, till at last the utmost distance rushes along at an equal speed, behind all the stems of the shrubs and the trees, and keeps up with you.

So is it truly in life. My childhood seems as near to me now as it was when I was twenty—nearer, I sometimes think; but the years of my early manhood have rushed by like that ribbon and are half swallowed by oblivion.

This line of thought threw me back into heavier moods. And yet, since now I banished the hardest of all thoughts hard to bear, I could not help succumbing to the influence of Nature's merry mood. I did so even more than I liked. I remember that, while driving through the beautiful natural park that masks the approach to the one-third-way town from the south, I as much as reproached myself because I allowed Nature to interfere with my grim purpose of speed. Half intentionally I conjured up the vision of an infinitely lonesome old age for myself, and again the sudden palpitation in my veins nearly prompted me to send my horses into a gallop. But instantly I checked myself. Not yet, I thought. On that long stretch north, beyond the bridge, there I was going to drive them at their utmost speed. I was unstrung, I told myself; this was mere sentimentalism; no emotional impulses were of any value; careful planning only counted. So I even pulled the horses back to a walk. I wanted to feed them shortly after reaching the stable. They must not be hot, or I should have trouble.

Then we turned into the main street of the town. In front of the stable I deliberately assumed the air of a man of leisure. The hostler came out and greeted me. I let him water the horses and waited, watch in hand. They got some hay, and five minutes after I had stopped, I poured their oats into the feeding boxes.

Then to the drug store—it was locked. I hunted the druggist all over town for nearly twenty minutes. Everybody had seen him a short while ago; everybody knew exactly where he had been a minute before; but nobody could discover him just then. I worked myself into a veritable frenzy of hurry. The moisture began to break out all over my body. I rushed back to the livery stable to tell the hostler to hitch up again—and there stood the druggist, looking my horses over! I shall not repeat what I said.

Five minutes later I had what I wanted, and after a few minutes more I walked my horses out of town. It had taken me an hour and fifty minutes to make the town, and thirty-five minutes to leave it behind.

One piece of good news I received before leaving. While I was getting into my robes and the hostler hooked up, he told me that no fewer than twenty-two teams had that very morning come in with cordwood from the northern correction line. They had made a farm halfway to town by nightfall of the day before; the rest they had gone that very day. So there would be an unmistakable trail all the way, and there was no need to worry over the snow.

I walked the horses for a while; then, when we were swinging round the turn to the north, on that long, twenty-mile grade, I speeded them up. The trail was good: that just about summarizes what I remember of the road. All details were submerged in one now, and that one was speed. The horses, which were in prime condition, gave me their best. Sometimes we went over long stretches that were sandy, under that inch or so of new snow, with sand blown over the older drifts from the fields—stretches where under ordinary circumstances I should have walked my horses—at a gallop. Once or twice we crossed bad drifts with deep holes in them, made by horses that were being wintered outside and that had broken in before the snow had hardened down sufficiently to carry them. There, of course, I had to go slowly. But as soon as the trail was smooth again, the horses would fall back into their stride without being urged. They had, as I said, caught the infection. My yearning for speed was satisfied at last.

Four sights stand out.

The first is of just such bunches of horses that were being brought through the winter with practically no yard feeding at all; and consequently their healthy outdoor looks and their velvety rumps were very conspicuous as they scattered away from the trail on our approach. Several times we dashed right in among them, and I had to shout in order to clear the road. They did not like to leave the firm footing on the trail, where they fed by pawing away the snow on both sides and baring the weeds. Sometimes a whole bunch of them would thunder along in a stampede ahead of us till they came to a cross-trail or to a farmyard; there we left them behind. Sometimes only one of them would thus try to keep in front, while the rest jumped off into the drifts; but, being separated from his mates, he would stop at last and ponder how to get back to them till we were right on him again. There was, then, no way to rejoin those left behind except by doing what he hated to do, by getting off the trail and jumping into the dreaded snow, thus giving us the right of way. And when, at last, he did so, he felt sadly hampered and stopped close to the trail, looking at us in a frightened and helpless sort of way while we dashed by.

The next sight, too, impressed me with the degree to which snow handicaps the animal life of our plains. Not more than ten feet from the heads of my horses a rabbit started up. The horses were going at a gallop just then. There it jumped up, unseen by myself until it moved, ears high, eyes turned back, and giving a tremendous thump with its big hind feet before setting out on its wild and desperate career. We were pretty close on its heels and going fast. For maybe a quarter of a mile it stayed in one track, running straight ahead and at the top of its speed so that it pulled noticeably away. Every hundred yards or so, however, it would slow down a little, and its jumps, as it glanced back without turning —by merely taking a high, flying leap and throwing its head aloft—would look strangely retarded, as if it were jumping from a sitting posture or braking with its hind feet while bending its body backward. Then, seeing us follow at undiminished speed, it would straighten out again and dart away like an arrow. At the end of its first straight run it apparently made up its mind that it was time to employ somewhat different tactics in order to escape. So it jumped slantways across the soft, central cushion of the trail into the other track. Again it ran straight ahead for a matter of four or five hundred yards, slowing down three or four times to reconnoitre in its rear. After that it ran in a zigzag line, taking four or five jumps in one track, crossing over into the other with a gigantic leap, at an angle of not more than thirty degrees to its former direction; then, after another four or five bounds, crossing back again, and so on. About every tenth jump was now a high leap for scouting purposes, I should say. It looked breathless, frantic, and desperate. But it kept it up for several miles. I am firmly convinced that rabbits distinguish between the man with a gun and the one without it. This little animal probably knew that I had no gun. But what was it to do? It was caught on the road with us bearing down upon it. It knew that it did not stand a chance of getting even beyond reach of a club if it ventured out in the deep, loose snow. There might be dogs ahead, but it had to keep on and take that risk. I pitied the poor thing, but I did not stop. I wished for a cross-trail to appear, so it would be relieved of its panic; and at last there came one, too, which it promptly took.

And as if to prove still more strikingly how helpless many of our wild creatures are in deep snow, the third sight came. We started a prairie chicken next. It had probably been resting in the snow to the right side of the trail. It began to run when the horses came close. And in a sudden panic as it was, it did the most foolish thing it possibly could do: it struck a line parallel to the trail. Apparently the soft snow in which it sank prevented it from taking to its wings. It had them lifted, but it did not even use them in running as most of the members of its family will do; it ran in little jumps or spurts, trying its level best to keep ahead. But the horses were faster. They caught up with it, passed it. And slowly I pulled abreast. Its efforts certainly were as frantic as those of the rabbit had looked. I could have picked it up with my hands. Its beak was open with the exertion—— the way you see chickens walking about with open beaks on a swooningly hot summer day. I reached for the whip to lower it in front of the bird and stop it from this unequal race. It cowered down, and we left it behind. . . .

We had by that time reached the narrow strip of wild land which separated the English settlements to the south from those of the Russian Germans to the north. We came to the church, and like everything else it rushed back to the rear; the school on the correction line appeared.

Strangely, school was still on in that yellow building at the corner. I noticed a cutter outside, with a man in it, who apparently was waiting for his children. This is the fourth of the pictures that stand out in my memory. The man looked so forlorn. His horse, a big, hulking farm beast, wore a blanket under the harness. I looked at my watch. It was twenty-five minutes past four. Here, in the bush country, where the pioneers carve the farms out of the wilderness, the time kept is often oddly at variance with the time of the towns. I looked back several times, as long as I could see the building, which was for at least another twenty minutes; but school did not close. Still the man sat there, humped over, patiently waiting. It is this circumstance, I believe, which fixed in my memory the exact hour at which I reached the correction line.

Beyond, on the first mile of the last road east, there was no possibility of going fast. This piece was blown in badly. There was, however, always a trail over this mile-long drift. The school, of course, had something to do with that. But when you drive four feet above the ground, with nothing but uncertain drifts on both sides of the trail, you want to be chary of speeding your horses along. One wrong step, and a horse might wallow in snow up to his belly, and you would lose more time than you could make up for in an hour's breathless career. A horse is afraid, too, of trotting there, and it takes a great deal of urging to make him do it.

So we lost a little time here; but when a mile or so farther on we reached the bush, we made up for it. This last run of five or six miles along the correction line consisted of one single, soft, smooth bed of snow. The trail was cut in sharply and never drifted. Every successive snowfall was at once packed down by the tree-fellers, and whoever drove along, could give his horses the lines. I did so, too, and the horses ran.

I relaxed. I had done what I could do. Anxiety there was hardly any now. A drive of more than forty miles, made at the greatest obtainable speed, blunts your emotional energies. I thought of home, to be sure, did so all the time; but it was with expectation now, with nothing else. Within half an hour I should know. . . .

Then the bush opened up. The last mile led along between snow-buried meadows, school and house in plain view ahead. There lay the cottage, as peaceful in the evening sun as any house can look. Smoke curled up from its chimney and rose in a nearly perpendicular column. I became aware of the colder evening air, and with the chill that crept over me I was again overwhelmed by the pitifully lonesome looks of the place.

Mostly I shouted when I drew near to tell of my coming. To-day I silently swung up through the shrubby thicket in which the cottage and the stable behind it lay embedded, and turned in to the yard. As soon as the horses stopped, I dropped the lines, jerked the door of the cutter back, and jumped to the ground.

Then I stood transfixed. That very moment the door of the cottage opened. There stood my wife, and between her knee and the door-post a curly head pushed through, and a child's voice shouted, "Daddy, come to the house! Daddy, come to the house!"

A turn to the better had set in sometime during the morning. The fever had dropped, and quickly, as children's illness will come, it had gone. But the message had sped on its way, irrevocable and, therefore, unrevoked. My wife, when she told me the tale, thought, well had she reason to smile, for had I not thus gained an additional holiday?

Chapter 7

SKIES AND SCARES

W E had had a "soft spell" over a week-end, and on Monday it had been followed by a fearful storm—snow-storm and blizzard, both coming from the southeast and lasting their traditional three days before they subsided. On Thursday, a report came in that the trail across the wild land west of Bell's corner was closed completely— in fact, would be impassable for the rest of the winter. This report came with the air of authority; the man who brought it knew what he was talking about; of that I had no doubt. For the time being, he said, no horses could possibly get through.

That very day I happened to meet another man who was habitually driving back and forth between the two towns. "Why don't you go west?" he said. "You angle over anyway. Go west first and then straight north." And he described in detail the few difficulties of the road which he followed himself. There was no doubt, he of all men should certainly know which was the best road for the first seventeen miles. He had come in from that one-third-way town that morning. I knew the trails which he described as summer-roads, had gone over them a good many times, though never in winter; so, the task of finding the trail should not offer any difficulty. Well and good, then; I made up my mind to follow the advice.

On Friday afternoon everything was ready as usual. I rang off at four o'clock and stepped into the hall. And right there the first thing went wrong.

Never before had I been delayed in my start. But now there stood three men in the hall, prominent citi-

zens of the town. I had handed my resignation to the
school board; these men came to ask me that I reconsider. The board, so I had heard, was going to accept
my decision and let it go at that. According to this com-
mittee the board did not represent the majority of the
citizens in town. They argued for some time against my
stubbornness. At last, fretting under the delay, I put it
bluntly. "I have nothing to reconsider, gentlemen. The
matter does no longer rest with me. If, as I hear, the
board is going to accept my resignation, that settles the
affair for me. It must of necessity suit me or I should not
have resigned. But you might see the board. Maybe they
are making a mistake. In fact, I think so. That is not
my business, however." And I went.

The time was short enough in any case; this cut it
shorter. It was five o'clock before I swung out on the
western road. I counted on moonlight, though, the fickle
luminary being in its first quarter. But there were clouds
in the north and the weather was by no means settled.
As for my lights, they were useless for driving so long
as the ground was completely buried under its sheet of
snow. On the snow there form no shadows by which you
can recognize the trail in a light that comes from between the two tracks. So I hurried along.

We had not yet made the first three miles, skirting
meanwhile the river, when the first disaster came. I
noticed a rather formidable drift on the road straight
ahead. I thought I saw a trail leading up over it—I
found later on that it was a snowshoe trail. I drove
briskly up to its very edge; then the horses fell into a
walk. In a gingerly kind of way we started to climb.
And suddenly the world seemed to fall to pieces. The
horses disappeared in the snow, the cutter settled down,
there was a sharp snap, I fell back—the lines had
broken. With lightning quickness I reached over the
dashboard down to the whiffle-trees and unhooked one

each of the horses' traces. That would release the others, too, should they plunge. For the moment I did not know what they were doing. There was a cloud of dust-dry snow which hid them. Then Peter emerged. I saw with horror that he stood on Dan who was lying on his side. Dan started to roll over; Peter slipped off to the right. That brought rebellion into Dan, for now the neck yoke was cruelly twisting his head. I saw Dan's feet emerging out of the snow, pawing the air: he was on his back. Everything seemed convulsed. Then Peter plunged and reared, pulling Dan half-way up; that motion of his released the neck-yoke from the pole. The next moment both horses were on their feet, head by head now, but facing each other, apparently trying to pull apart; but the martingales held. Then both jumped clear of the cutter and the pole; and they plunged out, to the rear, past the cutter, to solid ground.

I do not remember how I got out; but after a minute or so I stood at their heads, holding them by the bridles. The knees of both horses shook, their nostrils trembled; Peter's eye looked as if he were going to bolt. We were only a hundred yards or so from a farm. A man and a boy came running with lanterns. I snapped the halter ropes into the bit rings and handed the horses over to the boy to be led to and fro at a walk so as to prevent a chill; and I went with the man to inspect the cutter. Apparently no damage was done beyond the snapping of the lines. The man, who knew me, offered to lend me another pair, which I promptly accepted. We pulled the cutter out backwards, straightened the harness, and hitched the horses up again. It was clear that, though they did not seem to be injured, their nerves were on edge.

The farmer meanwhile enlightened me. I mentioned the name of the man who had recommended the road. Yes, the road was good enough from town to town.

This was the only bad drift. Yes, my adviser had passed here the day before; but he had turned off the road, going down to the river below, which was full of holes, it is true, made by the ice-harvesters, but otherwise safe enough. The boy would go along with his lantern to guide me to the other side of the drift. I am afraid I thought some rather uncharitable things about my adviser for having omitted to caution me against this drift. What I minded most was, of course, the delay.

The drift was partly hollow, it appeared; the crust had thawed and frozen again; the huge mass of snow underneath had settled down. The crust had formed a vault, amply strong enough to carry a man, but not to carry horse and cutter.

When in the dying light and by the gleam of the lantern we went through the dense brush, down the steep bank, and on to the river, the horses were every second ready to bolt. Peter snorted and danced, Dan laid his ears back on his head. But the boy gave warning at every open hole, and we made it safely. At last we got back to the road, I kept talking and purring to the horses for a while, and it seemed they were quieting down.

It was not an auspicious beginning for a long night-drive. And though for a while all things seemed to be going about as well as I could wish, there remained a nervousness which, slight though it seemed while unprovoked, yet tinged every motion of the horses and even my own state of mind. Still, while we were going west, and later, north into the one-third-way town, the drive was one of the most marvellously beautiful ones that I had had during that winter of marvellous sights.

As I have mentioned, the moon was in its first quarter and, therefore, during the early part of the night high in the sky. It was not very cold; the lower air was quiet, of that strange, hushed stillness which in southern countries is the stillness of the noon hour in midsummer—

when Pan is frightened into a panic by the very quiet. It was not so, however, in the upper reaches of the atmosphere. It was a night of skies, of shifting, ever-changing skies. Not for five minutes did an. aspect last. When I looked up, after maybe having devoted my attention for a while to a turn in the road or to a drift, there was no trace left of the picture which I had seen last. And you could not help it, the sky would draw your eye. There was commotion up there—operations were proceeding on a very vast scale, but so silently, with not a whisper of wind, that I felt hushed myself.

A few of the aspects have persisted in my memory, but it seems an impossible task to sketch them.

I was driving along through open fields. The trail led dimly ahead. Huge masses of snow with sharp, immovable shadows flanked it. The horses were very wide awake. They cocked their ears at every one of the mounds; and sometimes they pressed rump against rump, as if to reassure each other by their mutual touch.

About half way up from the northern horizon there lay a belt of faintest luminosity in the atmosphere—no play of northern lights—just an impalpable paling of the dark blue sky. There were stars, too, but they were not very brilliant. Way down in the north, at the edge of the world, there lay a long, low-flung line of cloud, black, scarcely discernible in the light of the moon. And from its centre, true north, there grew out a monstrous human arm, reaching higher and higher, up to the zenith, blotting the stars behind it. It looked at first—in texture and rigid outline—as the stream of straw looks that flows from the blower of a threshing machine when you stand straight in its line and behind it. But, of course, it did not curve down. It seemed to stretch and to rise, growing more and more like an arm with a clumsy fist at its end, held inconceivably straight and unbending. This cloud, I have no doubt, was forming right then by con-

densation. And it stretched and lengthened till it ob-
scured the moon.

Just then I reached the end of my run to the west. I
was nearing a block of dense poplar bush in which
somewhere two farmsteads lay embedded. The road
turned to the north. I was now exactly south of and in
line with that long, twenty-mile trail where I had startled
horses, rabbit, and partridge on the last described drive.
I believe I was just twenty-five miles from the northern
correction line. At this corner where I turned I had to
devote all my attention to the negotiating of a few bad
drifts.

When I looked up again, I was driving along the
bottom of a wide road gap formed by tall and stately
poplars on both sides—trees which stood uncannily still.
The light of the moon became less dim, and I raised my
eyes. That band of cloud—for it had turned into a band
now, thus losing its threatening aspect—had widened
out and loosened up. It was a strip of flocculent, sheepy-
looking little cloudlets that suggested curliness and
innocence. And the moon stood in between like a good-
natured shepherd in the stories of old.

For a while I kept my eyes on the sky. The going was
good indeed on this closed-in road. And so I watched
that insensible, silent, and yet swift shifting of things in
the heavens that seemed so orderly, pre-ordained, and
as if regulated by silent signals. The clouds lost their
sheeplike look again; they became more massive; they
took on more substance and spine, more manliness, as
it were; and they arranged themselves in distinct lines.
Soldiers suggested themselves, not soldiers engaged in
war, but soldiers drilling in times of peace, to be reviewed, maybe, by some great general. That central
point from which the arm had sprung and which had
been due north had sidled over to the northwest; the
low-flung line along the horizon had taken on the shape

of a long wedge pointing east; farther west it, too, looked more massive now—more like a rather solid wall. And all those soldier-clouds fell into a fan-shaped formation —into lines radiating from that common central point in the northwest. This arrangement I have for many years been calling "the tree." It is quite common, of course, and I read it with great confidence as meaning "no amount of rain or snow worth mentioning." "The tree" covered half the heavens or more, and nowhere did I see any large reaches of clear sky. Here and there a star would peep through, and the moon seemed to be quickly and quietly moving through the lines. Apparently he was the general who reviewed the army.

Again there came a shifting in the scenes. It looked as if some unseen hands were spreading a sheet above these flocculent clouds—a thin and vapoury sheet that came from the north and gradually covered the whole roof of the sky. Stars and moon disappeared; but not, so far, the light of the moon; it merely became diffused— the way the light from an electric bulb becomes diffused when you enclose it in a frosted globe. And then, as the sheet of vapour above began to thicken, the light on the snow became dim and dimmer, till the whole of the landscape lay in gloom. The sheet still seemed to be coming, coming from the north. But no longer did it travel away to the south. It was as if it had brought up against an obstacle there, as if it were being held in place. And since there was more and more of it pressing up—it seemed rather to be pushed now—it telescoped together and threw itself into folds, till at last the whole sky looked like an enormous system of parallel clothes-lines over all of which one great, soft, and loose cloth were flung so that fold after fold would hang down between all the neighbouring pairs of lines; and between two folds there would be a sharply converging, upward crease. It being night, this arrangement, common in grey

daylight, would not have shown at all, had it not been
for the moon above. As it was, every one of the infolds
showed an increasingly lighter grey the higher it folded
up, and like huge, black udders the outfolds were hanging down. This sky, when it persists, I have often found
to be followed within a few days by heavy storms. To-
night, however, it did not last. Shifting skies are never
certain signs, though they normally indicate an unsettled
condition of the atmosphere. I have observed them after
a blizzard, too.

I looked back over my shoulder, just when I emerged
from the bush into the open fields. And there I became
aware of a new element again. A quiet and yet very distinct commotion arose from the south. These cloth-
clouds lifted, and a nearly impalpable change crept over
the whole of the sky. A few minutes later it crystallized
into a distinct impression. A dark grey, faintly luminous,
inverted bowl stood overhead. Not a star was to be seen
above, nor yet the moon. But all around the horizon
there was a nearly clear ring, suffused with the light of
the moon. There, where the sky is most apt to be dark
and hazy, stars peeped out—singly and dimly only—I
did not recognize any constellation.

And then the grey bowl seemed to contract into
patches. Again the change seemed to proceed from the
south. The clouds seemed to lift still higher, and to
shrink into small, light, feathery cirrus clouds, silvery on
the dark blue sky—resembling white pencil shadings.
The light of the moon asserted itself anew. And this
metamorphosis also spread upward, till the moon her-
self looked out again, and it went on spreading northward till it covered the whole of the sky.

This last change came just before I had to turn west
again for a mile or so in order to hit a trail into town.
I did not mean to go on straight ahead and to cut across
those radiating road lines of which I have spoken in a

former part. I knew that my wife would be sitting up and waiting till midnight or two o'clock, and I wanted to make it. So I avoided all risks and gave my attention to the road for a while. I had to drive through a ditch and through a fence beyond, and to cross a field in order to strike that road which led from the south through the park into town. A certain farmstead was my landmark. Beyond it I had to watch out sharply if I wanted to find the exact spot where according to my informant the wire of the fence had been taken down. I found it.

To cross the field proved to be the hardest task the horses had had so far during the night. The trail had been cut in deep through knee-high drifts, and it was filled with firmly packed, freshly blown-in snow. That makes a particular bad road for fast driving. I simply had to take my time and to give all my attention to the guiding of the horses. And here I was also to become aware once more of the fact that my horses had not yet forgotten their panic in that river drift of two hours ago. There was a strawstack in the centre of the field; at least the shape of the big, white mound suggested a strawstack; and the trail led closely by it. Sharp shadows showed, and the horses, pricking their ears, began to dance and to sidle away from it as we passed along its southern edge.

But we made it. By the time we reached the park that forms the approach to the town from the south, the skies had changed completely. There was now, as far as my eye would reach, just one vast, dark-blue, star-spangled expanse. And the skies twinkled and blazed down upon the earth with a veritable fervour. There was not one of the more familiar stars that did not stand out brightly, even the minor ones which you do not ordinarily see oftener than, maybe, once or twice a year —as, for instance, Vega's smaller companions in the constellation of the Lyre, or the minor points in the cluster of the Pleiades.

I sometimes think that the mere fact of your being on a narrow bush-road, with the trees looming darkly to both sides, makes the stars seem brighter than they appear from the open fields. I have heard that you can see a star even in daytime from the bottom of a deep mine-pit if it happens to pass overhead. That would seem to make my impression less improbable, perhaps. I know that not often have the stars seemed so much alive to me as they did that night in the park.

And then I came into the town. I stayed about forty-five minutes, fed the horses, had supper myself, and hitched up again.

On leaving town I went for another mile east in the shelter of a fringe of bush; and this bush kept rustling as if a breeze had sprung up. But it was not till I turned north again, on the twenty-mile stretch, that I became conscious of a great change in the atmosphere. There was indeed a slight breeze, coming from the north, and it felt very moist. Somehow it felt homely and human, this breeze. There was a promise in it, as of a time, not too far distant, when the sap would rise again in the trees and when tender leaflets would begin to stir in delicate buds. So far, however, its more immediate promise probably was snow.

But it did not last, either. A colder breeze sprang up. Between the two there was a distinct lull. And again there arose in the north, far away, at the very end of my seemingly endless road, a cloud-bank. The colder wind that sprang up was gusty; it came in fits and starts, with short lulls in between; it still had that water-laden feeling, but it was now what you would call "damp" rather that "moist"—the way you often feel winter-winds along the shores of great lakes or along sea-coasts. There was a cutting edge to it—it was "raw." And it had not been blowing very long before low-hanging, dark, and formless cloud-masses began to scud up from the north to the zenith. The northern lights, too, made their appearance again about that time. They formed an arc very far to the south, vaulting up behind my back, beyond the zenith. No streamers in them, no filtered rays and streaks, nothing but a blurred luminosity high above the clouds and—so it seemed—above the atmosphere. The northern lights have moods, like the clouds —moods as varied as theirs—though they do not display them so often nor quite so ostentatiously.

We were nearing the bridge across the infant river. The road from the south slopes down to this bridge in a rather sudden, S-shaped curve, as perhaps the reader remembers. I still had the moonlight from time to time, and whenever one of the clouds floated in front of the crescent, I drove more slowly and more carefully. Now there is a peculiar thing about moonlight on snow. With a fairly well-marked trail on bare ground, in summertime, a very little of it will suffice to indicate the road, for there are enough rough spots on the best of trails to cast little shadows, and grass and weeds on both sides usually mark the beaten track off still more clearly, even though the road lead north. But the snow forms such an even expanse, and the trail on it is so featureless, that these signs are no longer available. The light itself also is too characterless and too white and too nearly of the same quality as the light reflected by the snow to allow of judging distances delicately and accurately. You seem to see nothing but one vast whiteness all around. When you drive east or west, the smooth edges of the tracks will cast sharply defined shadows to the north, but when you drive north or south, even these shadows are absent, and so you must entirely rely on your horses to stay on the trail. I have often observed how easily my own judgment was deluded.

But still I felt so absolutely sure that I should know when I approached the bridge that, perhaps through over-confidence, I was caught napping. There was another fact which I did not take sufficiently into account at the time. I have mentioned that we had had a "soft spell." In fact, it had been so warm for a day or two that the older snow had completely iced over. Now, much as I thought I was watching out, we were suddenly and quite unexpectedly right on the downward slope before I even realized that we were near it.

As I said, on this slope the trail described a double curve, and it hit the bridge at an angle from the west. The first turn and the behaviour of the horses were what convinced me that I had inadvertently gone too far. If I had stopped the horses at the point where the slope began and then started them downward at a slow walk, we should still have reached the bridge at too great a speed; for the slope had offered the last big wind from the north a sheer brow, and it was swept clean of new snow, thus exposing the smooth ice underneath; the snow that had drifted from the south, on the other hand, had been thrown beyond the river, on to the lower northern bank; the horses skidded, and the weight of the cutter would have pushed them forward. As it was, they realized the danger themselves, for when we turned the second curve, both of them stiffened their legs and spread their feet in order to break the momentum of the cutter; but in spite of the heavy calks under their shoes they slipped on all fours, hardly able to make the bend on to the bridge.

They had to turn nearly at right angles to their last direction, and the bridge seemed to be one smooth sheet of ice. The moon shone brightly just then; so I saw exactly what happened. As soon as the runners hit the iced-over planks, the cutter swung out sideways; the horses, however, slipping and recovering, managed to make the turn. It was a worth-while sight to see them strike their calks into the ice and brace themselves against the shock which they clearly expected when the cutter started to skid. The latter swung clear of the bridge—you will remember that the railing on the east side was broken away—out into space, and came down with a fearful crash, but right side up, on the steep north bank of the river—just at the very moment when the horses reached the deep, loose snow beyond which at least gave them a secure footing. They had gone along the diagonal of the bridge, from the southwest corner, barely clearing the rail, to the northeast corner where the snow had piled in to a depth of from two to five feet on the sloping bank. If the ground where I hit the bank had been bare, the cutter would have splintered to pieces; as it was, the shock of it seemed to jar every bone in my body.

It seemed rather a piece of good luck that the horses bolted; the lines held; they pulled me free of the drift on the bank and plunged out on the road. For a mile or two we had a pretty wild run; and this time there was no doubt about it, either, the horses were thoroughly frightened. They ran till they were exhausted, and there was no holding them; but since I was on a clear road, I did not worry very much. Nevertheless, I was rather badly shaken up myself; and if I had followed the good advice that suggested itself, I should have put in for some time at the very next farm which I passed. The way I see things now, it was anything rather than safe to go on. With horses in the nervous condition in which mine were I could not hope any longer to keep them under control should a further accident happen. But I had never yet given in when I had made up my mind to make the trip, and it was hard to do so for the first time.

As soon as I had the horses sufficiently in hand again, I lighted my lantern, got out on the road, and carefully looked my cutter over. I found that the hardwood lining of both runners was broken at the curve, but the steel shoes were, though slightly bent, still sound. Fortunately the top had been down, otherwise further damage would have been sure to result. I saw no reason to discontinue the drive.

Now after a while—when the nervousness incident upon the shock which I had received subsided—my interest in the shifting skies revived once more, and again I began to watch the clouds. The wind was squally, and the low, black vapour-masses overhead had coalesced into a vast array of very similar but yet distinct groups. There was still a certain amount of light from the moon, but only just enough to show the texture and the grouping of the clouds. Hardly ever had I seen, or at least consciously taken note of, a sky that with its blackness and its massed multitudes of clouds looked so threatening, so sinister, so much like a battle-array. But way up in the northeast there were two large areas quite suffused with light from the north. They must have been thin cloud-layers in whose upper reaches the northern lights were playing. And these patches of light were like a promise, like a word of peace arresting the battle. Had it not been for these islands of light, I should have felt depressed when I looked back to the road.

We were swinging along as before. I had rested the horses by a walk, and to a casual observer they would have seemed to be none the worse for their fling at running away. But on closer scrutiny they would again have revealed the unmistakable signs of nervous tension. Their ears moved jerkily on the slightest provocation. Still, the road was good and clear, and I had no apprehensions.

Then came the sudden end of the trail. It was right in front of a farmyard. Clearly, the farmer had broken the last part of the road over which I had come. The trail widened out to a large, circus-shaped flat in the drifts. The snow had the ruffled appearance of being thoroughly tramped down by a herd of cattle. On both sides there were trees—wild trees—a-plenty. Brush lined the narrow road-gap ahead; but the snow had piled in level with its tops. This had always been rather a bad spot, though the last time I had seen it the snow had settled down to about half the height of the shrubs. I stopped and hesitated for a moment. I knew just where the trail had been. It was about twenty-five feet from the fence of the field to the east. It was now covered under three to four feet of freshly drifted-in snow. The drift seemed to be higher towards the west, where the brush stood higher, too. So I decided to stay as nearly as I could above the old trail. There, even though we might break through the new snow, the older drifts underneath were likely to be firm enough.

We went ahead. The drift held, and slowly we climbed to its summit. It is a strange coincidence that just then I should have glanced up at the sky. I saw a huge, black cloud-mass elbowing its way, as it were, in front of those islands of light, the promise of peace. And so much was I by this time imbued with the moods of the skies that the disappearance of this mild glimmer sent a regret through my very body. And simultaneously with this thrill of regret there came—I remember this as distinctly as if it had been an hour ago—the certainty of impending disaster. The very next moment chaos reigned. The horses broke in, not badly at all; but as a consequence of their nervous condition they flew into a panic. I held them tight as they started to plunge. But there was no guiding them; they were bound to have things their own way altogether. It seemed as if they had lost their road-sense, too, for instead of plunging at least straight ahead, out on the level trail, they made, with irresistible bounds and without paying the slightest attention to the pull of the lines, towards the east. There the drift, not being packed by any previous traffic, went entirely to pieces under their feet. I had meanwhile thrown off my robes, determined at all costs to bring them to a stop, for I knew, if I allowed them to get away with me this time, they would be spoiled for any further drives of mine.

Now just the very fraction of a second when I got my feet up against the dashboard so as to throw my whole weight into my pull, they reared up as if for one tremendous and supreme bound, and simultaneously I saw a fence post straight under the cutter pole. Before I quite realized it, the horses had already cleared the fence. I expected the collision, the breaking of the drawbar and the bolting of the horses; but just then my desperate effort in holding them told, and dancing and fretting they stood. Then, in a flash, I mentally saw and understood the whole situation. The runners of the cutter, still held up by the snow of the drift which sloped down into the field and which the horses had churned into slabs and clods, had struck the fence wire and, lifting the whole of the conveyance, had placed me, cutter and all, balanced for a moment to a nicety, on top of the post. But already we began to settle back.

I felt that I could not delay, for a moment later the runners would slip off the wire and the cutter fall backward; that was the certain signal for the horses to bolt. The very paradoxicality of the situation seemed to give me a clue. I clicked my tongue and, holding the horses back with my last ounce of strength, made them slowly dance forward and pull me over the fence. In a moment I realized that I had made a mistake. A quick pull would have jerked me clear of the post. As it was, it slowly grated along the bottom of the box; then the cutter tilted forward, and when the runners slipped off the wire, the cutter with myself pitched back with a frightful knock against the post. The back panel of the box still shows the splintered tear that fence post made. The shock of it threw me forward, for a second I lost all purchase on the lines, and again the horses went off in a panic. It was quite dark now, for the clouds were thickening in the sky. While I attended to the horses, I reflected that probably something had broken back there in the cutter, but worst of all, I realized that this incident, for the time being at least, had completely broken my nerve. As soon as I had brought the horses to a stop, I turned in the knee-deep snow of the field and made for the fence.

Half a mile ahead there gleamed a light. I had, of course, to stay on the field, and I drove along, slowly and carefully, skirting the fence and watching it as closely as what light there was permitted.

I do not know why this incident affected me the way it did; but I presume that the cumulative effect of three mishaps, one following the other, had something to do with it; the same as it affected the horses. But more than that, I believe, it was the effect of the skies. I am rather subject to the influence of atmospheric conditions. There are not many things that I would rather watch. No matter what the aspect of the skies may be, they fascinate me. I have heard people say, "What a dull day!"—or, "What a sleepy day!"—and that when I was enjoying my own little paradise in yielding to the moods of cloud and sky. To this very hour I am convinced that the skies broke my nerve that night, that those incidents merely furnished them with an opportunity to get their work in more tellingly.

Of the remainder of the drive little needs to be said. I found a way out of the field, back to the road, drove into the yard of the farm where I had seen the light, knocked at the house, and asked for and obtained the night's accommodation for myself and for my horses.

At six o'clock next morning I was on the road again. Both I and the horses had shaken off the nightmare, and through a sprinkling, dusting fall of snow we made the correction line and finally home in the best of moods and conditions.

THE AUTHOR

FREDERICK PHILIP GROVE was born in 1871 in southern Sweden. In Toronto in 1892 he learned of the death of his father and the collapse of the family fortunes. For twenty years he roamed the continent, working as a farmhand in the West. In 1912 he became a school teacher in Manitoba and continued in that profession until 1924, when deafness obliged him to resign. Meanwhile he had married very happily, but a great grief was added to the trials of financial stringency and uncertain health when his young daughter died in 1927. Two years later, he and his wife left the West; they settled in Simcoe, Ontario, and it was there that Grove died in 1948.

He is the author of eight published novels, an autobiography, three volumes of essays and sketches, and many short stories. In 1934 the Royal Society of Canada awarded him the Lorne Pierce Gold Medal for Literature, and in 1945 he received an honorary degree from the University of Manitoba. His best work—with the exception of his autobiography, *In Search of Myself* (1946), which won him a Governor-General's prize, and an early autobiographical novel entitled *A Search for America*—has the Canadian West as its setting and inspiration. It includes *Over Prairie Trails, The Turn of the Year*, and four of the novels: *Settlers of the Marsh, Our Daily Bread, The Yoke of Life*, and *Fruits of the Earth*.

THE NEW CANADIAN LIBRARY